P9-DET-370

PELÉ

PELÉ

A Biography

Lew Freedman

GREENWOOD BIOGRAPHIES

GREENWOOD

AN IMPRINT OF ABC-CLIO, LLC
Santa Barbara, California • Denver, Colorado • Oxford, England

JOHN TYLER
COMMUNITY COLLEGE LIBRARY
CHESTER, VIRGINIA 23831

DISCARD

GV
942.7
.P42
F74
2014

Copyright 2014 by ABC-CLIO, LLC

All rights reserved. No part of this publication may be reproduced, stored in a
retrieval system, or transmitted, in any form or by any means, electronic, mechanical,
photocopying, recording, or otherwise, except for the inclusion of brief quotations in
a review, without prior permission in writing from the publisher.

Library of Congress Cataloging-in-Publication Data

Freedman, Lew.
  Pelé : a biography / Lew Freedman.
    pages cm. — (Greenwood biographies)
  Includes index.
  ISBN 978-1-4408-2980-2 (hardback) — ISBN 978-1-4408-2981-9 (ebook) (print)
1. Pelé, 1940–   2. Soccer players—Brazil—Biography.   I. Title.
  GV942.7.P42F74   2014
  796.334092—dc23
  [B]   2013027228

ISBN: 978-1-4408-2980-2
EISBN: 978-1-4408-2981-9

18 17 16 15 14   1 2 3 4 5

This book is also available on the World Wide Web as an eBook.
Visit www.abc-clio.com for details.

Greenwood
An Imprint of ABC-CLIO, LLC

ABC-CLIO, LLC
130 Cremona Drive, P.O. Box 1911
Santa Barbara, California 93116-1911

This book is printed on acid-free paper ∞

Manufactured in the United States of America

DISCARD

CONTENTS

SERIES FOREWORD

In response to school and library needs, ABC-CLIO publishes this distinguished series of full-length biographies specifically for student use. Prepared by field experts and professionals, these engaging biographies are tailored for students who need challenging yet accessible biographies. Ideal for school assignments and student research, the length, format, and subject areas are designed to meet educators' requirements and students' interests.

ABC-CLIO offers an extensive selection of biographies spanning all curriculum-related subject areas including social studies, the sciences, literature and the arts, history and politics, and popular culture, covering public figures and famous personalities from all time periods and backgrounds, both historic and contemporary, who have made an impact on American and/or world culture. The subjects of these biographies were chosen based on comprehensive feedback from librarians and educators. Consideration was given to both curriculum relevance and inherent interest. Readers will find a wide array of subject choices from fascinating entertainers like Miley Cyrus and Lady Gaga to inspiring leaders like John F. Kennedy and Nelson Mandela, from the greatest athletes of our time like Michael Jordan and Muhammad Ali to the most amazing success stories of our day like J. K. Rowling and Oprah.

While the emphasis is on fact, not glorification, the books are meant to be fun to read. Each volume provides in-depth information about the subject's life from birth through childhood, the teen years, and adulthood. A thorough account relates family background and education, traces personal and professional influences, and explores struggles, accomplishments, and contributions. A timeline highlights the most significant life events against an historical perspective. Bibliographies supplement the reference value of each volume.

INTRODUCTION

In the 1970s, when soccer great Pelé came to the United States to play for the New York Cosmos of the North American Soccer League, American newspaper readers and television watchers were informed that he was the best-known person in the world.

Since soccer was not considered a major sport in the country at that time—indeed, one of the main reasons the Brazilian luminary chose to come out of retirement—the somewhat egocentric American public had trouble believing or understanding that claim.

But it was undoubtedly true. What the American audience failed to comprehend was the grip soccer had on the rest of the world. Throughout South and Central America, Europe and Africa, soccer was king. Soccer was not only the most important sport in most of the nations on earth, it was also deeply entwined in the fabric of the cultures of most of those countries.

As the best player in the world, and indisputably the best of all time, Pelé transcended national boundaries. He was a human deity to any soccer-following country on the planet. The president of the United States may have been the most powerful man on earth, but Pelé was recognized by peasants in deserts and tribesmen in jungles.

For many of the poor of the earth, soccer was the only game. It was so inexpensive to play that even those that lived in impoverished communities or countries could rustle up a ball, or a facsimile of a ball, something made by themselves that was suitable to kick around.

Pelé was such a special player that even those not invested or well-educated in the sport could pick him out of a scrum anonymously. His skills shone that brightly. If fans knew of his personal history, rising from poor circumstances himself, they could identify with it. And for those of black skin, for those of minority status, resentful of previous white colonialism, it did not hurt any that Pelé was also dark-skinned.

Over the decades, from the time Pelé made his debut as a teenager on the world scene by representing his country in the World Cup of 1958, Pelé's stature and status steadily grew, and his fame did so commensurately as well. He was the only man in the history of the sport to score 1,000 goals—a figure that denoted him as being at least part-magician.

In addition, the Pelé who showed himself to the Brazilian people and the world at large was gracious and engaging. He signed autographs endlessly. He smiled enthusiastically in triumph and was humble in defeat. He gave of himself and sought to set an example as a great man, as well as a great player, without ever stating so explicitly.

The player known as Pelé was born Edson Arantes do Nascimento, though outside of signature requirements on legal documents, his use of that full and more cumbersome name long ago fell into disuse. Pelé became Pelé as a youth, and the origin of the name continues to baffle him. It was as if a new name was needed to apply to someone demonstrating impossibly new skills.

In Brazil, Pelé was not only acclaimed as a national hero for bringing so much honor to his home country through its favorite sport, but was proclaimed a national treasure, as if he were a concrete monument built in the heart of the country.

Through salary and endorsements, at one time, Pelé was also the richest athlete in the world. Yet, like some of his sporting contemporaries, he was taken advantage of and keenly felt the loss of many of his assets. He had the fortitude to start over and rebuild and long after playing his final game for Brazil in 1971, he remains a wildly popular figure and very much a national treasure.

The entirety of Pelé's soccer involvement from his youth until his early 30s was built around competing for the national team in the biggest matches and for his Brazilian club team. Many times, Pelé fielded offers to play for wealthy clubs in other countries, but always turned them down to remain affiliated with Santos, the only club of his prime years.

It was only after Pelé retired from the sport, feeling himself slowing down a little bit, in the mid-1970s while in his mid-30s, that he was persuaded to get back into action for an American team. It was an extraordinary coup for the New York Cosmos, talking Pelé out of retirement and into their lineup. Considerable money changed hands, but that was not the sole motivator for Pelé—he had brushed aside bigmoney deals more than once.

The most important aspect of the deal for Pelé was a chance to broaden the imprint of soccer on the world's richest country, inhabited by millions of sports-loving people. Pelé came to New York to teach Americans about soccer and to show Americans what the sport he called the "beautiful game" could be like when played at a high level.

During his years with the Cosmos, Pelé uplifted the sport and his name recognition in the one major country that had pretty much previously ignored him. It did not happen overnight, but Americans did embrace soccer more and more passionately, the American national team has been a regular World Cup qualifier, and an American soccer league is thriving and periodically attracts some of the best foreigners onto team rosters.

When he retired, Pelé had accumulated an amazing 1,281 goals. It is a monumental achievement unsurpassed and unapproached. That number alone stands as testimony to Pelé's greatness, even among those born too late to watch him perform his ballet on the field. It will also explain to some Pelé's exalted status and his return to the news pages in his seventies, as the country that he long ago provided with intense national pride through its national soccer team will thrust him to the forefront as the world's eyes turn to Brazil over the next few years.

Brazil has committed itself to the daunting task of readying the nation to become host to the world's two largest sporting events. The World Cup soccer tournament is headed to Brazil in 2014 and the Summer Olympic Games will be played there in 2016.

Front and center in the public eye, at first, lobbying for those events to be awarded to Brazil, but also speaking to the Brazilian people about the glorious opportunity they have to showcase their land, Pelé is once again representing his country on the world stage.

Now in his seventies, Pelé is too old to participate in soccer games anymore, but when the Games come to him in Brazil, surely he will stand alone as the symbol of his country's sporting history. He will no doubt be wearing a wide smile as sports lovers visit the country he so many times made so proud.

TIMELINE: EVENTS IN THE LIFE OF PELÉ

1940   Born October 23, in Tres Coracoes, Brazil, as Edson Arantes do Nascimento.

1942   Family moves to Bauru, Brazil.

1956   Scouted by and signed by Santos club junior team.

1957   Promotion to Santos top level team.

1958   Becomes overnight sensation in 1958 World Cup in Sweden as Brazil wins championship.

1962   Brazil defends World Cup in Chile.

1966   Marries Rosemeri Cholhy. Competes in third World Cup in England, though Brazil loses.

1967   Daughter Kelly Cristina born.

1969   Scores historic 1,000th goal.

1970   Leads Brazil to record third World Cup championship in Mexico.

1970   Son Edson born.

1971   Retires from international soccer competition with national team.

1974   Retires from Santos club competition.

1974   Declines to compete in World Cup.

1975	Comes out of retirement to play for New York Cosmos and boost American soccer.
1976	Leads Cosmos to playoffs and North American Soccer League attendance records.
1977	Leads Cosmos to NASL championship, more attendance records.
1977	October 1, retires from soccer.
1977	United Nations certificate presentation as Citizen of the World.
1978	Daughter Jennifer born.
1978	Divorces Rosemeri.
1978	Begins work for UNICEF.
1994	Marries second wife, Assiria Seixas Lemos.
1995	Works as Brazil's minister of sport.
1996	Twins, son Joshua and daughter Celeste, are born.
1999	Chosen Athlete of the 20th Century by International Olympic Committee.
2000s	Acts as goodwill ambassador for Brazilian soccer and country as whole.
2008	Divorces Assiria Seixas Lemos.
2012	Appears at closing ceremony of the 2012 Summer Olympics London as part of transition to Brazil quadrennial.

Chapter 1

EARLY LIFE

From early on in life, the boy admired and revered his soccer-playing father. Where they came from, skill in soccer was a prized attribute, and the boy's dad was very good at the sport.

As he grew into childhood, the boy cherished the time his father spent kicking the ball around with him, and whenever he got the chance to watch his father play for his club team, the boy was spellbound by the spectacle and enthusiastic in his cheering.

Truly, the most influential figure in the development of the boy's soccer skills was close to home, in the home itself. In this way, Edson Arantes do Nascimento became enraptured by the sport he came to define. Dondinho, the father, and Dona Celeste, his mother, who did not even like soccer, were too poor to equip their son with the necessary equipment, but he found a way.

The oldest child in the family was born on October 23, 1940, in the Brazilian community of Tres Coracoes, which in English means Three Hearts. Three Hearts is located in the state of Minas Gerais and the boy who would become Pelé was born into a hard life. Despite the solicitude and efforts of Dondinho, the family was impoverished. Dona Celeste was from Three Hearts and she met Pelé's father when

Dondinho was stationed there for army service. Dona Celeste was only 15 when they married and only 16 when she gave birth to Pelé.

For several years, it was a challenge to provide enough food for the family. The purchase of soccer shoes, or even a ball, was out of the question. They were luxury items. So, as was common among the local boys in such communities, those with the will to play the most popular sport in the country improvised. Dondinho took an old sock and filled it to bulging with rags. It took on a roundish shape and was good enough for a five-year-old.

Dondinho was passionate about soccer and was an accomplished enough player to be the star of the local side in the town. However, it was a team that was not wealthy and could not afford to pay its players more than starvation wages. That has become a phrase over the decades in professional sport, used to disparage a cheapskate organization, yet in this case, it was almost literally accurate.

Still, Dondinho was spotted as an up-and-coming talent and in 1942, when Pelé was two years old, he was hired to play for the Atletico Mineiro in the larger state capital. This was a terrific opportunity and promised Dondinho much greater exposure and a better financial deal. Fate was cruel to him almost immediately, however. In Dondinho's first

Raised in poverty, growing up in a small town, Pelé attributed his level-headed approach to stardom and his early soccer prowess to the influence of his parents, father Dondinho and mother Dona Celeste. (AP Photo)

game with his new club, a collision with an opposing player ruined him. Dondinho suffered torn ligaments in his knee and the injury left him with a permanent limp. His new team cut him and paid for his return transportation to Three Hearts.

Surgery to repair such injuries among sports figures was in its infancy at best, and Dondinho did not trust it. Eschewing an operation, he let the knee heal on its own through rest, which proved inadequate. From then on, he was not the same quality player, though he kept trying.

This incident is what turned Pelé's mother, Dona Celeste, against soccer. She called the sport "nonsense."[1] Her husband's love for the sport remained undiminished, but his earning capacity had been eroded—at least from soccer. Two years passed, but against the odds, Dondinho received another offer. The new deal combined suiting up for a soccer team named FC Bauru, and working a public service job. The family moved.

While this seemed to be a grass-is-greener solid opportunity, once again, Dondinho's circumstances were compromised by bad luck. New ownership took over the team and while he remained a member of the squad, the public service position—which Dondinho was counting on, evaporated. The family was expanding. Pelé now had a brother named Jair and a sister named Maria Lucia. His mother's brother, Uncle Jorge, lived with the family, as did his grandmother Ambrosina. They had moved to a strange city for the chance to better their situation, but the rules changed on them, putting tremendous stress on Dondinho's shoulders.

"And so we existed," Pelé said. "But as I grew up I began to learn what poverty was. Poverty is a curse that depresses the mind, drains the spirit, and poisons life. There was a great deal of love in that small house, love that overcame much of the hardship."[2]

Pelé's earliest days were shaped by his immediate family and its moves, as is the case in almost all families. Pelé found his daily life to be fun and full of play opportunities with neighboring children after the move to Bauru. He made his comments about early-life poverty from hindsight, looking back at his youth from the perspective of adulthood. But as has been echoed many times by those who grew up with little, they did not notice their poverty-stricken circumstances all of the time because all of those who lived nearby were in the same situation.

Their economic lifestyles were similar, so there was no jealousy, and there was no longing to possess fancy possessions that no one else in the area had either.

There is no question, though, that later in life, when he was a richer man, Pelé gave considerable thought to what poverty means, even if he did not recognize it when he was a kid.

"Poverty was wondering what would happen if we couldn't raise the money for the firewood," he said. "Poverty was begrudging and even hating each stick of kindling that went into the hungry maw of that stove, and being forced to feed it, anyway. Poverty, in short, is being robbed of self-respect and self-reliance. Poverty is fear. Not fear of death, which, though inevitable, is reasonable. It is fear of life. It is a terrible fear."[3]

His home area was heavy with children and they all played together outside. Brazil was an ethnic melting pot, so there were white, black, and mixed heritage children, all hanging out together with no tensions. Pelé was dark-skinned, black, but many, many citizens of Brazil are of mixed race. What the kids did to fill their time was play circus, building one in Pelé's backyard, and other simple games like that. The future soccer great remembers the kids playing together from dawn to dusk. Then, the boys turned to "futebol" instead of what they now felt were frivolous games. Soccer is more commonly referred to as football in most of the rest of the world besides the United States.

That first soccer ball was indeed made of socks filled with rags, but as Pelé remembers it, sometimes the stuffing was old newspapers, and then string was used to tie the "ball" together.

"As we became more proficient in the game, and as we grew bigger, we would use more and more stuffing, making a bigger and heavier ball," Pelé said. "Some of the socks we used for our balls, or for their stuffing, were taken from clotheslines before the owner was aware that he had contributed, but we felt our greater need justified the borrowing. A man could always walk around without socks, but a kid needed something to kick."[4]

From the moment he began to play soccer, Pelé very much enjoyed the sport. But he did not look at it as a career opportunity. He was determined to become an airplane pilot, not a professional soccer player. Soccer, however, was very much the national sport of the country. In the United States, just about every little boy of a certain age grew up playing baseball on the local fields, or even in the streets. In Brazil, everyone gravitated toward soccer.

Later, after he became a national icon, Pelé looked back and said the theme of those years of his youth with regard to the sport might well have been defined by this philosophy: "If it moves, kick it. If it doesn't move, kick it and make it move. If it's too big to kick, trade it in on something smaller and kick that."[5]

Brazil itself is the largest country in land mass and population in South America. As the fifth largest country in the world, Brazil's borders contain 3.3 million square miles. It was smaller in population when Pelé was growing up, but now has nearly 200 million people. During the age of exploration, Brazil came under the sway of Portugal and that European country ruled the warmer, more tropical possession from 1500 to 1815. Complete independence was accomplished in 1822, but the main language of Brazil, unlike most of the countries on the continent which speak Spanish, is Portuguese.

Part of the nation's wealth, as well as its name, stems from a plentiful supply of brazilwood trees, which thrive mainly along the abundant coastline. A rain rich country, Brazil is often hot and humid and its area includes part of the Amazon Rainforest. Brazil has also long been a religious country, with a strong leaning toward Roman Catholicism.

When it comes to sport, Brazil has some support for auto racing, basketball, and volleyball, but compared to soccer, those allegiances are minor. That is one thing that has not changed in Pelé's time. Pelé's own contributions strengthened Brazil's belief in its standing in the soccer world and the country has won a record five World Cup titles. Again, Pelé must be thanked for his contributions on that front.

However, the boy who was kicking a rag ball around was quite a different person than the magnificent athlete who performed such feats. That was all in the future as the ragtag youngster was simply playing soccer for fun with his friends. When Edson was a little boy, his father called him "Dico," but that is only remembered in family lore. No one outside the household really used the name. The child was about 10 years old, playing soccer with his friends, when he was anointed with a new nickname.

The great puzzlement of Pelé's childhood, career, and remarkable ascension to sports superstar is that the name he became known to the world by apparently came out of thin air. The name Pelé was applied to him by his compatriots in the streets, yet no one claims that he was the originator. Even more confusing, it did not grow out of a personal trait or an athletic one that the player can think of, since the word is not even an official word in Portuguese. The famed and unique name was simply conjured up one day and it stuck.

"I have no idea where the name came from, or who started it," Pelé said, "because it has no meaning in Portuguese, or any other language, as far as I know." Years after he acquired the name, Pelé returned to the Bauru area, looked up old friends, and asked them to explain to him anything they remembered about the creation of the name. He basically came up empty. "But they don't have a clue as to its origin, or exactly when it started, either. They say it just began one day and after that it stuck because it seemed to fit, whatever it means."[6]

Pelé did offer one story that he admitted sounded like a reach as a possible way that he acquired his new name. A teammate of his father's in club play was the goalie called Bile. When he was very little, Pelé was around that team and he dabbled in playful goal-tending. Just maybe, he was referred to as "Little Bile" when he stopped a shot and he misunderstood and it morphed into Pelé.

"Either I changed it myself, according to my Uncle Jorge, or it was because of my thick Minas Gerais accent," Pelé said.[7] Such an explanation, even from Pelé's mouth directly, sounds far-fetched because he was not generally called Pelé until years later.

Most likely, Pelé is Pelé just because it was a unique name for a unique player. Of course, at the time, no one could have imagined that this kid called Pelé would make the name world famous and that it would be enduring. If there are other Pelés out there, it is almost certainly because they have been named after this Pelé.

Ironically, when Pelé was first called Pelé by others, he took it as somewhat of an insult because they were ignoring his given name. He even got into fights about it, but when he lost the fights, he gave up trying to change anyone's mind. If his fisticuff prowess had perhaps been more violent and successful, it is possible that the world's greatest soccer player would be known as "Ed" for short.

Pelé began school as a youngster along with the other children he roamed the streets with, but he did not enjoy sitting in classrooms. He felt like a prisoner compared to the freedom offered playing outdoors.

It wasn't that he didn't understand his studies; he just did not apply himself—something he regretted later in life. While teachers sought to fill his head with facts on geography, mathematics, and the social sciences, his mind was fixated on only one topic—soccer. He spent his school days daydreaming about playing soccer.

It had not taken much to steer Pelé away from his first career goal of becoming a pilot. This seemed like a sort of fantasy career option, not so dissimilar from an American boy initially declaring he wanted to be a cowboy, a police officer, or firefighter, some job that offered considerable action. When he found the time, Pelé used to make his way to the local Aero Club and indulge in thoughts of wearing goggles and the leather clothing that pilots appeared so impressive in—he thought that would be him some day. That is, until one day at the Aero Club, he and some friends were peeking through a window and watched as attempts were made to revive a dead man who had crashed a glider. Afterward, Pelé had nightmares about the scene and spiked his own plans to become any kind of flyer.

School bored Pelé and he disliked his main teacher. He prevailed on his family to let him drop out and go to work after he completed the fourth grade. He, sometimes in the company of his friends, contemplated moneymaking schemes.

Before he even dropped his formal schooling, Pelé skipped doing his homework in favor of working as a shoeshine boy. He went door-to-door in the neighborhood—his mother forbade him from roaming too far from home—but was not a great success. The first group effort to make money with his friends involved stealing peanuts from a warehouse and selling them. Pelé and his gang made this pay and they used the proceeds for soccer uniforms—minus the shoes. Although Pelé went along with this program initially, all he saw in his future was the likelihood of being caught, sent to jail, and being labeled a criminal. He quickly backed away from this idea.

Instead, Pelé became involved with collecting soccer cards and putting them into albums. They were traded for a long-coveted ball. Eventually, Pelé took a job as a cobbler's apprentice. His pay was slightly more than $2 a month, most assuredly, a humbling salary.

Pelé continued to play soccer with his friends as often as possible. However, their poverty restricted them to playing barefoot. None of them could afford real soccer shoes. The team name was September 7, but they were called "The Shoeless Ones." By the time Pelé reached the age of 10, his father saw the spark of talent in him and began giving him instructions and taking him to fields for workouts. Most importantly, he taught his son how to use both feet on the pitch.

A local tournament was being sponsored by the mayor's office of Bauru and Pelé and his teammates wanted to play. The father of three players offered to at last shoe the team if it would accept him as its coach. The man did not pay for new shoes out of his own pocket, but persuaded another team to surrender its old shoes. For Pelé and his friends, that did not matter one bit—it was like acquiring magic slippers.

The team name changed to Little America and at 12 Pelé was the youngest player. Playing before a crowd of 5,000 fans, Pelé scored the winning goal and his team captured the Junior Victory Cup. To the youngsters involved, it might as well have been the real World Cup.

Championship day was one of the most memorable days of Pelé's life. There was actually cash distributed to the team. The 36 cruzeiros' value did not really amount to much, but his appreciative teammates gave it all to him because of his extraordinary play. Dona Celeste, who was not on the premises, and who never watched her son play, made him divide it up anyway. But the monetary reward was not the biggest thing.

"Of all the many memories I have of that glorious day, two things stand out," Pelé said later. "The crowd calling my name, 'Pelé! Pelé!' in a constantly growing chant, until I found myself no longer hating the name, but actually beginning to like it, and my father holding me tightly after the match and saying, 'You played a beautiful match.'"[8]

This marked a turning point in Pelé's life. His playing well in an organized tournament led to increased exposure of the kind that piques the curiosity of scouts on the prowl. An influential Brazilian soccer figure, Valdemar de Brito, had been on the national scene for years. He was a player for Brazil in the 1934 World Cup and coached the Bauru team that Dondinho competed in. Pelé's father did not have to talk him up once de Brito saw the boy play. He was not yet 12 years old, but de Brito saw his potential. "I couldn't believe that such a young boy was able to perform some of the moves, as well as the tricks with the ball that Pelé was doing," de Brito said.[9]

When scouting youngsters, there is always a risk. One never knows if the boy will maintain his devotion and passion to the sport. One must project growth and physical development as well. Is the player really that talented, or does he excel because he is only playing against his friends who are OK competitors, but not among the most talented? Yet, de Brito was convinced that Pelé was the genuine article, that he was not just a boy wonder, but would become an adult wonder. There was something about him, in the manner he played, in the maturity of his game that stood out and seemed to herald greater things to come.

"I can honestly say that in all the years I have been observing promising young soccer players, no youngster ever had such an impact on me as this youngster," de Brito said. "And I found it hard to believe that he was only 12 years old. Some of the moves he made reminded me of the greats of the game, and I myself, who was considered to be a pretty good junior player in my early days, had to admit that at the same number of years he was far ahead of me."[10]

De Brito got a junior Bauru club team started with Pelé as the centerpiece. No longer shoeless, Pelé shone. But de Brito pined for a return to a bigger city and moved home to Sao Paulo to take a job coaching professional players. Pelé was offered a position on another club team, Radium, and while he was the only amateur on the squad, he led the team with 40 goals. The more people who saw Pelé play, the more apparent it was that the lad had a future in the game.

While he was perfecting his craft, Pelé worked part-time at a train station selling meat pies to travelers. Strangely, the growing boy came up short on his inventory more than once. He told his patrons they must have been stolen, though it was generally conceded that the always-underfed seller probably sampled the wares. Pelé returned to school and completed more class work, essentially through the equivalent of the eighth grade.

Pelé was 15 when de Brito reappeared. He had kept track of Pelé from afar and now that he was a little bit older and a little bit stronger, he felt it was time for him to move up in the Brazilian soccer ranks. De Brito wanted to take Pelé away from home and sign him up for the prominent Santos club. Pelé's mother, Dona Celeste, did not like this plan. She did not want her baby to move away and, even worse, it seemed to her, he was going to be casting his lot in the world of professional soccer—a realm for which she had no affection.

Santos was located on the water south of Sao Paulo more than 300 miles away. At first, his mother refused to give her permission.

De Brito arranged for the Santos team president to call Pelé's parents and provide assurances that he would be well-cared for and protected because of his tender age, as well as being fairly compensated. Despite her misgivings, and through her tears, Dona Celeste gave Pelé her blessing. Tugging at her was the realization that her son was not a great student who would only find opportunities limited in the white-collar world, and she most certainly did not want to see him spend his career as a cobbler's assistant. "To me, you are still a little boy," Dona Celeste said, "but everyone else seems to think you're grown up. You were never a good student and I don't want you sewing boots for the rest of your life."[11]

The deal was sealed. Dondinho and Pelé took the train to Santos. Pelé's family was not wealthy enough to own a car. He had traveled nowhere, so even the train ride was new to him. Alas, when the train began moving, Pelé endured the first experience informing him that he was entering a new world—he got sick to his stomach from the motion. He informed his father that he wanted to get off. Dondinho had to calm Pelé's nerves and stomach both as the train rolled on. The distance from Bauru to Santos was 312 miles, but it might as well have been 10,000 miles measured in terms of Pelé's previous travel experiences, and it might as well have been 10,000 miles measuring the distance he was moving up in his soccer career, too.

Upon Dondinho's and Pelé's arrival in Santos, they were accompanied by de Brito to make an immediate visit to the stadium for a game. Once the game ended, Pelé was introduced to his new coach and his new surroundings. De Brito had done some selling job about Pelé's qualities and potential, even going so far as to interest Santos by telling team representatives, "This boy is going to be the greatest player in the world!"[12]

The coach was Luis "Lula" Alonso and he greeted Pelé by saying, "So you're the famous Pelé."[13] De Brito's glowing endorsement had preceded him.

When Pelé met the players, all of whom were older, Dondinho pleasantly but somewhat urgently asked those among them that he knew to take care of his son for him. It would have been easy, and not so uncommon, for the players to resent a newcomer thrust upon them with such advance notices, and treat him roughly as an initiation. But they did not do so. They made Pelé feel welcome and rather treated him as a younger brother.

Pelé was a center-forward, positioned in the middle of the field, and a position that in the hands (or in this case, the feet) of a well-developed player with creativity could provide opportunities for scoring goals. At first, Pelé was homesick being on his own and nervous about scrimmaging with his older teammates. He was skinny in size at 130 pounds, and also had a skinny resume compared to these players. While Pelé had the speed and the moves to blend in, he was not strong enough to fend off defenders. Lula noticed this right away and realized his young prodigy might get soundly battered by opponents. Hence, part of Pelé's training program was to eat a lot—it was an assignment. For someone who had been raised in poverty, where there was sometimes a shortage of filling food, this was a blessing. This was beyond his imagination. Although his diet was watched so that he did not eat solely junk food, Pelé was supposed to beef up. Until then, while practicing with the "A" team, his competition was limited.

Little brother care or not, Pelé was still required to perform the tasks of a new kid in town, constantly being told by the older players to fetch them coffee. Much later in life, Pelé always remembered how he gained another nickname for a short time. The Santos players would say, "Get me a coffee, kid, and don't spare the gasolina." The guys began calling him "Gasolina."[14]

Despite his passion for soccer, despite being invited to join a men's team, Pelé was nearly overcome by his homesickness at times. Once, he packed his suitcase and was sneaking out of the very basic accommodations he shared (with bunk beds and a nail on the wall for clothes) at 5:00 A.M. to catch a train home. Only, he was intercepted by a team assistant named Big Sabu, who ran the kitchen. He had a brief discussion with the boy, buoyed his spirits, and Pelé retreated to his room.

During this learning period, Pelé represented Santos' junior team in games and acquitted himself well. After watching him for a time, team officials decided he was well worth keeping and they wanted to sign him to a contract. However, because he was underage, this was illegal.

There was, though, a "wink-and-a-nod" procedure that such teams followed that was also referred to as "a contract in the drawer." After some negotiation that did include a Pelé visit home, his parents agreed to a deal beginning in April 1957 of 5,000 cruzeiros a month.

Lest anyone believe that young Pelé was going to get rich off of this arrangement, 4,000 of those cruizeiros were earmarked for his parents and he was given 1,000 cruzeiros as spending money. As Pelé later described it, in his first pro contract, he was essentially playing for $10 a month. When he turned 16, he got a raise to $15 a month, his years still outpacing his dollars.

Until then, Dona Celeste was able to fool herself into believing that Pelé's stay with Santos was temporary and that he would soon be coming home to stay and live with his family again. Once the agreement was inked, it was obvious Pelé was on his way in the professional ranks and most likely would never live at home again. It was not hard to see why she still considered her oldest son to be a child. At the time, Pelé stood just over five feet tall and his weight was up to 145 pounds. Yet, Pelé believed in himself and his ability to succeed in soccer, going farther than his father had, and Santos officials who saw players come and go every day also recognized that they had something special in Pelé, even if he was still raw and young.

The first game Pelé represented Santos in was a junior game in which he scored three goals, whetting the appetite of the coaching staff. But in another junior game, one that counted more, Pelé had an off day. Everything he tried that day went wrong. He not only missed a penalty shot, but received rough treatment from the crowd, being booed off the field. After the game, Pelé cried in his room and a few hours later he once again packed his possessions and, in order to live down the humiliation he felt from the game, planned to run home again. Coincidentally and somewhat remarkably, he ran into the very same team official, Big Sabu, who had stopped him the first time. The very persuasive older man again talked Pelé into sticking around.

De Brito, Pelé's discoverer, of course heard about his prodigy's periodic near-flights and one time he gave him a talking-to, reminding Pelé that this was a huge opportunity to make money and eventually become a star and that it would do him no good to duck the limelight and return home to his challenging family circumstances. In retrospect,

Pelé believed this lecture was good for him. "That day I became a man," he said.[15]

At last, Pelé was elevated to the first team for a game. In soccer, not all games are considered equal. Some involve other nations, some involve league play, some involve club rivals, and some are termed "friendlies" to distinguish them as being of lesser importance. Pelé made his debut with the top Santos team in a friendly against a team named Cubatao. What a debut it was! If the Santos players had been wondering what the fuss was all about with this teenager joining their ranks, Pelé showed them that day. He scored four goals in a 6–1 victory.

While this was the equivalent of winning an exhibition game, it was still an unforgettable performance. Opportunity awaited Pelé and it came in the form of injury to another Santos player. Pelé donned the No. 10 center-forward jersey against a team from Sweden. He obtained his first professional goal against the Corinthians Santo Andre club and once Pelé got started, he kept rolling. In his first 11 games for the top-level Santos team, he scored 15 goals.

The boy was just 16 years old, but he was on his way to becoming the greatest goal scorer in world soccer history. And before Pelé turned 17, soccer fans throughout Brazil would know his name. When he played before 100,000 spectators in Rio de Janeiro's great Maracana Stadium, scoring a colorful goal, and leading Santos to a 1–0 triumph over America of Rio, the fans gave him an ovation. He had arrived.

NOTES

1. Harry Harris, *Pelé: His Life and Times* (New York: Welcome Rain Publishers, 2001), p. 14.

2. Ibid., p. 15.

3. Pelé and Robert L. Fish, *My Life and the Beautiful Game* (New York: Doubleday & Company, 1977), p. 15.

4. Ibid.

5. Ibid., p. 16.

6. Harris, p. 19.

7. Pelé, *My Life in Pictures* (New York: Simon & Schuster, 2008), p. 14.

8. Harris, p. 23.

9. Joe Marcus, *The World of Pelé* (New York: Mason/Charter, 1976), p. 15.

10. Ibid., p. 16.

11. Bill Gutman, *Pelé* (New York: Grosset & Dunlap, 1976), p. 31.

12. Harris, p. 26.

13. Ibid., p. 27.

14. Ibid., p. 28.

15. François Thebaud, *Pelé* (New York: Harper & Row Publishers, 1976), p. 9.

Chapter 2

EARLY FAME

Pelé's coach Lula was an astute man. He recognized that his teenaged phenomenon possessed great skill, but he also wanted to carefully nurture it. The boy was naturally impatient, seeking as much time on the field as possible. But Lula played him sparingly at first, careful to put him in situations where he was likely to succeed. He did not want Pelé to be physically overpowered by the men—and they were men—that marked him on defense. That meant choosing the right teams for Pelé's starts.

However, it took only a very short time for Pelé to prove he could play against anyone. He may have been slight in stature, but he made up for it with lightning speed, incredible reflexes, and his remarkable football control. When Pelé dribbled up-field, his mastery of the ball could be breathtaking. It was as if the ball was an extension of his foot.

Once Pelé's Santos teammates and the fans saw him maneuvering around opposing defenses, there was no keeping him on the bench. Everyone wanted to see more of this unknown player. He was just 16 at the time, but Pelé became a regular for one of Brazil's top clubs. What was obvious to those who saw him play was that Pelé possessed a special instinct for making plays, for finding openings, and finding teammates with passes. It was the type of instinct which could not be taught, but which was natural. In essence, Pelé's feel for the game was a gift. It was now up to him to determine what he would do with it.

It did not take very long for the homesick boy who kept trying to run away to mature into a top-notch player worthy of the regular starting center-forward position in Santos' lineup. And it did not take long for others to notice his talent. While making the starting lineup at Pelé's age was an achievement in itself, he did not merely run up and down the field as a background figure. In soccer, the center-forward is often the catalyst of the offense. The man who mans the spot must perform. He has the opportunity and responsibility to score, and if he cannot do so himself, he must assist his teammates. Making plays is what the role calls for and making plays is what Pelé delivered.

Once Pelé found his comfort zone in the Santos lineup, he soon found his comfort zone as an offensive juggernaut. As his shoulders broadened and his thigh muscles especially were thickened and grew more powerful, Pelé discovered that growing into the game came as readily as growing into his body.

Brazilian fans are connoisseurs of the game and when Santos followers realized how good he was, they embraced Pelé and cheered him wildly. Pelé made a move and the crowd "oohed." Pelé made another move and the crowd "ahhed." Pelé finished a play with a goal and the crowd roared. Soon enough, Pelé's name was appearing in newspaper accounts of games. That helped him become known beyond the boundaries of Santos and the league. Much was happening quickly. Only months earlier, Pelé was the little brother of the team, but now, he was practically leading it. Only months earlier, Pelé was being pushed around by the stronger, fully grown men in the league, but now, he was tricking the defenders out of their shoes as he bent the ball around them with his marvelous footwork. In all of his spare time, Pelé worked on getting stronger and being in better shape and in perfecting his passing with drills. He was turning Waldemar de Brito's faith into reality.

Playing part-time, Pelé demonstrated that he had a nose for the goal and that his foot could outsmart goalies' hands. It became obvious to Lula that Pelé needed to play all of the time and as soon as he inserted Pelé into the starting lineup for good, he began scoring like a pinball machine. Against Paulista, a major club rival, Pelé scored two goals.

Against Lavras, he scored four goals. In a tournament, he scored six goals in four games.

Unlike basketball or some other sports where points come in bushels, every goal scored in soccer is precious. Many games are settled by 1–0 or 2–1 counts. That makes the scoring of any goal subject to an emotional celebration. It was during one of his Santos club games his first year as a full-time professional when Pelé developed his signature goal-scoring celebration. It was not pre-planned, but visceral. The ball flew into the net and an exuberant Pelé punched his fist at the air in triumph. After that, he did it every time he scored a goal. Pelé scored a lot of goals in his career, so fans got to see the fist pump quite often.

Of course, defenders resented being shown up by this youngster and they became determined to stop him one way or the other. That meant physical play and illegal hits on Pelé's seemingly fragile body at times. Referees would or could only protect him so much. Otherwise, he had to take the pounding and prove that he was tough enough to play at a higher level.

Truly, Pelé's reputation was growing swifter than his body. The national team coach, Silvio Pirilo, was blown away by Pelé's skills and chose him to compete for Brazil against Argentina in July 1957. The national press was not impressed by his selection, with one comment being particularly memorable: "A 16-year-old playing against opponents as tough as Argentina . . . it's madness! Anyway, who is Pelé?"[1]

The rest of Brazil, which had not yet made Pelé's acquaintance, was about to find out. Brazil lost the grudge match to Argentina 2–1, but Pelé scored the only goal for his side. When the countries met again, this time with Brazil winning 2–0, he scored again.

There are times when an athlete arrives on the scene at just the right, fortunate moment. Saved from laboring in obscurity, taking years to battle to the top of his game, this athlete is a chosen one, recognized immediately for his talent and hurried along with no qualms because everyone who has caught a glimpse of him understands he will be great. Sometimes, those notions are proven false and the athlete fizzles. In Pelé's case, however, the assessments were all precisely on target. The young soccer player was as great as everyone said he was and once he was given entrée to the world stage, everyone knew it.

The World Cup soccer tournament is one of the world's greatest sporting spectacles. The only thing that can rival it are the Olympic Games. Held every four years since 1930 except for 1942 and 1946 because of World War II, the World Cup qualifiers begin at least a year before the final 32-team competition is conducted in one country. Qualifying by continent alone is extremely challenging, and for some nations is a prize in itself. Mere qualifying does not connote success in Brazil. Anything less than a championship is considered failure. At least partially due to Pelé's heroics at the height of his career, Brazil's five titles make the South American country the most successful of all those going into the 2014 event.

In 1958, the World Cup was hosted by Sweden. Brazil had qualified as one of the teams entered from its part of the world. However, the national team's roster was not set. That would not be finalized until the last minute because of potential injuries and current performances to be taken into consideration. The decision of who Brazil should name to play and who to take as its representatives rested with a selection committee, not the judgment of a single coach.

The method of notifying players they had been chosen was also a bit less personal than it would be now. Players learned their fate at the same time the very avid fan base learned who was on the roster. Because of the intense national interest, the announcement of the tentative roster was made over the radio. Pelé's reputation had grown, not simply in the view of those who had seen him play first-hand, which basically were fans of Santos and their opponents. It went beyond that because in 1958, he scored 87 goals. All one had to do is look at the number and recognize that this player who had been completely unknown to the Brazilian soccer world a year before was performing miraculous feats with his feet. That single number raised Pelé's profile and earned him the type of attention that could elevate him onto the national team even at a tender age.

Pelé was at home visiting his family in Bauru, listening to the radio, when he heard the announcement. He was shocked and delighted and said to Dona Celeste, "Mother, I've been invited to play with the Brazilian championship soccer team!"[2]

At the exact moment when the announcement was issued, Pelé was actually in the house alone, with the radio on as a backdrop for his entertainment. He did not know the broadcaster was going to talk about soccer. "When I heard the announcer say something about invitations to the Brazilian Selection . . . ," Pelé said, he turned his full attention to the subject. "I got up quickly and walked over, bending over the radio, listening intently. I didn't want to miss a word. When he started to rustle his papers before reading the list, I felt myself grow cold. I knew I wouldn't hear my name. I promised myself I wouldn't cry, or kick the furniture, or pound my head against the wall if I wasn't mentioned, but I wasn't sure."[3]

The fact that Pelé could even entertain notions that he, as a 16-year-old, might be chosen to participate in soccer's grand event seemed far-fetched. Only a year earlier, he had been a complete unknown outside of his neighborhood. Only months earlier, he had been a Santos back-up. His progress was fantastic. But in Brazil every single soccer player shared the same dream—of being one of the small number of players chosen to compete for his country in front of hundreds of thousands of spectators and hundreds of millions of radio and television followers. Pelé had burst upon the scene so recently, his name was not even yet known to all soccer fans. Despite the brilliance shown in this so-far magical season, it seemed a wild hope to believe he might be invited to play in the World Cup.

The names were uttered, one by one, the broadcaster drawing out his pronunciation of each player's name for drama. He did not rush through the list, but made long pauses between every name mentioned. One name ended in r and the r became rrrrr. About a half-dozen names into the list, Pelé heard his own name mentioned. He was stunned.

"I didn't even hear the rest," he said. "I found myself back in my chair, trembling violently, wondering if I had really heard it or had allowed my imagination to tell me what I wanted to hear. But the list was being repeated, and so was my name. And at that moment my mother walked into the room."[4]

Pelé was so emotional that his mother became concerned. She thought he was getting sick. Dona Celeste did not even realize the magnitude of what her shaking son was trying to tell her. She walked over to him and felt his forehead, trying to determine if he was running a fever.

A fever! Yes, it was a fever of sorts. Pelé's soccer fever had carried him to one of the highest honors he could attain and the nation's soccer fever focused on Pelé as some fans sought to learn about him and other fans debated the merits of whether such a young player was the right fit for this all-important team.

This was only the preliminary selection, the larger group from which 22 players would make the final selection for the actual World Cup participation. After some practices, the final roster would be shaped. The names mentioned on the radio constituted the list that Coach Vincente Feola would cull.

When it came time, Feola handled things differently. Those players whose names Feola mentioned aloud had to go home. Pelé's name was not among those uttered. He was a keeper. As he inwardly celebrated—because those who did not make the team were tremendously aggrieved right in front of him, some of them even crying—Pelé was equally astonished.

There was a firestorm of discussion nationally because not all supporters believed that the ideal squad had been selected. There was one particularly controversial cut from the Corinthians club, a player named Luisinho. Before the national team departed for Europe, it played a game against Corinthians in Sao Paulo. The fans booed their own national team for its harsh treatment of their favorite.

During the game, Pelé scored a goal, but more importantly, he was hit on a play as he dribbled the ball and twisted his right knee. He tried to continue playing on it, but crumpled to the turf. This was terrible timing. If the injury was a bad one and it seemed unlikely he would be able to play in Sweden, Pelé would be dropped from the team before departure and replaced on the roster. He was very worried about his status and his health.

The very first treatment of the knee problem was an ice pack. Given that he was representing the Brazilian national team, Pelé had first-rate care and attention. The team's masseur, Mario Americo, did not seem exceptionally concerned by the injury. "Don't worry about it, kid," Americo said. "Leave it to daddy. I'll have you chasing girls again in no time."[5]

There were some controversial allegations that it was possible a Corinthians player fouled Pelé on purpose in retaliation for teammate Luisinho being left off the team, but Pelé never made the charge. He wasn't sure exactly what happened, either at the time, or later, when he rethought the situation.

In 1958, Brazil—with young Pelé playing a significant role—won its first World Cup championship. Pelé helped lead his country to a record three World Cup titles during his career. (AP Photo)

Neither Feola's nor other Brazilian team officials' faith in Pelé wavered and he stayed on the team. Pelé, though, did not cease worrying about being pulled off the squad until he was on the plane to Europe. Then he continued worrying about his knee. It was a legitimate problem and he drew considerable attention from the team trainers. Pelé fretted nonstop. He had bucked the odds and been chosen for the national team, but to travel to Europe and be sidelined by injury seemed like a potentially very frustrating outcome. As a backdrop to his situation, Pelé knew that his own father's soccer career had been severely hampered by a knee injury.

Disappointed by his problem and inability to play, Pelé actually volunteered to be sent home and be replaced by another player. Team officials told him to soldier on right where he was. As a warm-up to the World Cup, Brazil played some friendly matches against countries that were not in the tournament. Pelé did not play. When the doctor examined him again, his commentary did not put Pelé at ease. The knee was not coming along as quickly as he had hoped.

There never was a diagnosis that indicated a severe injury, only a nagging one. Day after day, Pelé was treated with steaming hot towels until finally, the rest paid off and the knee was pronounced fit for competition. By then, Pelé had missed some of the early games of the Cup competition. The medical doctors said Pelé was good to go.

The team psychologist, almost in a parody of psychiatry, had the players draw pictures of humans and interpreted their readiness to play based on the sketches. Goofball reports accompanied the psychologist's analysis of the drawings. He determined from Pelé's rudimentary drawing that he was "obviously infantile" and "lacks the necessary fighting spirit."[6] He reported that Pelé should not be played. However, coach Feola rejected these comments as psycho-babble and went with his own instincts of what would work on the field.

Although, at times, Pelé grew quite discouraged over the main business of soccer and his incapacitation, he very much enjoyed being in a foreign country so different from Brazil and mingling with the athletes from all over the world. He also struck up a friendship with a young blonde white Swedish girl named Lena, whose company he kept on long walks from his team hotel.

"We would go out hand in hand, thrilled with each other's different color, happy to be together," Pelé said. "We were both 17, a very romantic age."[7] He never forgot Lena and decades later they met again briefly on one of the then-famed soccer great's world tours. During those idyllic, short weeks in Sweden, when Pelé and Lena mixed, Pelé was a boyish teenager with the world about to flower in front of him. His worldwide image and status changed from complete anonymity to being internationally admired within the same time period, before he left Sweden.

Brazil, one of the favorites, advanced to the quarterfinals with Pelé as a spectator. He was given the green light to play in his country's match against Wales. It was a tight game all of the way, scoreless at the half. This was unexpected. The Brazilians perhaps took Wales for granted, but the underdog team neutralized their best attacks. Not only had the Welsh goaltender Jack Kelsey played superbly, the Brazilians failed to finish off their best chances.

However, in the second half, the ball, and opportunity, bounced Pelé's way. He booted a shot into the net for a 1–0 lead. Pelé took a feed from Didi (it is Pelé's theory that Brazilians are given such long names at birth because many of them do not own very many possessions, but then names are all shortened for ease in speaking), and the net yawned open. Pelé, who was blessed with great peripheral vision, did not shoot immediately, however, because out of the corner of his eye, he saw the foot of a defender snaking in to block him. Demonstrating the type of flair and control of the ball that made his reputation, Pelé paused to bounce the ball lightly in the air as the swinging foot passed and missed, then let the ball drop to the ground before kicking it. At first, Pelé believed the shot was going to be stopped by the net-minder, but it hit a player's foot in the front of the goal and deflected in.

The moment the ball nestled into the net, Pelé and his mates celebrated wildly. Pelé ran around, kept jumping into the air, and screaming. He yelled "Goooooaaaaaalllllll!" as long and loudly as he could. He said he was "a maniac" in that moment. "I had to get rid of that tremendous pressure of relief, of joy, of I don't know what was inside of me! I was crying like a baby, babbling, while the rest of the team pummeled me, almost suffocating me. That was certainly my most unforgettable goal—my luckiest it has been said, possibly—but definitely my most unforgettable."[8]

That goal stood up as the game-winner, the only goal of the game. Brazil was on its way to the World Cup semifinals in a showdown against France. Young Pelé had waited through some anxious times to take his place on the field, but when he got his chance, he thanked his coach for his belief by scoring when his team needed him. The game lasted 90 minutes, as all soccer games do, but it felt like an eternity until Pelé scored and the Brazilians could deflect Wales' upset bid.

These are the types of games that go down in sporting history, but when players are in the middle of competing in a tournament, they do not have time to always savor the moment. That must wait until the tournament ends and the team travels home. That's because there is always another game ahead of them, another obstacle preventing their ascension to a championship. They must hurriedly refocus, come back to earth, as it were, to prepare for the next challenge.

However, Pelé was now in the limelight. Brazil had proceeded through the preliminary rounds of the Cup tournament with him nursing a sore knee. But once he was able to compete, he performed spectacularly. One goal at the right time can transform a soccer player's career and that happened to Pelé. From simply a name on the roster to the soccer fans in Sweden, he had suddenly become *the* name. After scoring against Wales, he was approached for autographs. Much to his surprise, other white Swedish girls flirted with him and actually ran their hands up and down his arms as if to see if the blackness of his skin might rub off. While he was the center of attention in Sweden, Pelé did wonder how the news of his critical goal was being handled back home—he hoped his family was proud of him.

If Pelé's game-winning goal against Wales struck a chord with the Brazilian public, he was about to up the ante and move into the realm of top-notch sporting hero with his showing against France. At this point in the tournament, Brazil had been a success story. Being among the final four teams playing in the Cup was an accomplishment. But once the Brazilians got so close to the trophy, they wanted to win it even more desperately. If they defeated France, the Brazilians would play for the title. If they lost, they would go home.

Although it is never quite true in team sports, the Brazil–France game was almost a solo act for Pelé. It was as if he personally opened a stage show as the main character, the leading man in a drama. Pelé's magnificence against France is sometimes overlooked, being sandwiched between scoring his game-winner against Wales and the championship contest against Sweden. But in his long World Cup career, representing his country four times on the grandest stage the sport has to offer, it is possible Pelé was never better than he was as a 17-year-old versus France. That day, he scored three goals and assisted on another as Brazil toppled France 5–2.

However, the result was not obtained as easily as it appeared from the final score. Brazil grabbed a 1–0 lead on a quick goal that Pelé believed would discourage the French right away. But France retaliated swiftly for a 1–1 tie. Then, without premeditation, and in an act that caught many of his older teammates by surprise, Pelé began dressing down the team, exhorting everyone to pick up his game and regain the lead. This verbal explosion, which caused fellow players to stare at him in disbelief, may well represent the moment when Pelé became the leader of the Brazilian team, for the remainder of that World Cup and for the years that followed.

Brazil took a 2–1 lead into the halftime break and made it 3–1 soon after. The Brazilians were in no danger after that. Feelings ran high during the game and a French player kicked Pelé in his sore knee. "I went down, hurting like the devil," he said, "and then rolled over to glare at the player with pure hatred."[9] Pelé wanted to fight the opposing player, but wasn't even sure his knee would support him. Plus, he did not want to get ejected from the game, so he refrained from retaliation. Teammate Didi calmed both him and the other Brazilians down, reminding them that the World Cup championship beckoned and that was much more important than becoming embroiled in fisticuffs with the French.

Pelé got his revenge a better way, by making a defender—the same one that kicked him on purpose—look like a fool. As the defender closed in, Pelé kicked the ball gently so that it sailed slightly over the head of the onrushing player. The ball landed just behind him, Pelé stepped around the player, and boomed a kick into the net for his final goal of the day. France's next job was to catch a plane back to Paris. Brazil's next assignment was toppling the host country's team in the World Cup final.

The championship game was scheduled for June 29, 1958, in Stockholm. As Pelé listened with pride to the Brazilian national anthem being played, he let his thoughts drift to his father, Dondinho, surely at home, tuned in to the game on the radio. Pelé wondered what his father was thinking about. Pelé gave himself a little bit of a laugh when he also realized that his mother, Dona Celeste, would be nowhere in the vicinity of the radio. She would steadfastly not listen to the contest, but she would stay informed as to Brazil's progress by a sort of telepathy. She would cock her ears in the direction of any yells, those produced by soccer fans in their reactions to goals scored or goals allowed. Somehow, she would figure out what occurred in the game, if her son was doing alright.

He was. More than alright, actually—a circumstance that would pretty much remain standard from that point on for the rest of his entire career.

While the Brazilians had gained a following among the World Cup fans in Sweden, the Swedish team was the host and clearly the favorite of the vast majority of the local fans. Pelé and his team, however, had other ideas about where the Cup should reside for the next four years.

If there was any worry on behalf of the Brazilians, it would be to ensure the impartiality of the refereeing so they were not victimized by any home cooking. The leaders of the delegation talked about this in the hours leading up to the final, but it may well have been posturing as an advance defensive measure more than any true concern.

Sweden's strategy was to score fast and try to hold the lead. The home team did get on the board first, scoring within the contest's first four minutes. It was the first time Brazil trailed during the entire tournament, but that deficit position did not last long. Five minutes later, the game was tied when Vava scored on a pass from Garrincha. Later in the first half, Vava scored again and it was 2–1 to Brazil after the initial 45 minutes of play.

Some 10 minutes into the second half, Pelé put his team on the scoreboard again with a stunning move. The play began with his back to the goaltender when a pass struck him in the thigh. Somehow, Pelé kept control of the ball instead of watching it trickle away. Then he spun around, fired on the goal and scored. Zagalo outran four defenders for another goal and the final score was 5–2 to Brazil when Pelé notched a second goal on a floating shot over the net-minder's head.

The play caught the Swedish goaltender so off-guard that he stood still, paralyzed by the brilliance of the shot. He later called the goal unlike any other he had tried to defend and said he doubted that he would ever have to face another unbelievable shot like it.

It was over. Brazil was the World Cup champion. There was a near riot of a celebration when the Brazilians realized their quest had been completed. Mario Americo sprinted into the goal-mouth to grab the ball from the last goal and refused to give it back to the officials. Players hugged and yelled. The emotions so overwhelmed Pelé that he almost fell to the ground.

He said he had "a strange feeling that I was going to faint. I felt my knees collapsing under me and reached out to prevent myself hitting the ground. And then I was being lifted, raised to the shoulders of my teammates, and being carried around the field."[10]

Even the greatest of players and coaches may go a lifetime in a sport without being carried around like royalty by their team. For this to happen to Pelé as a 17-year-old, a newcomer to the national team, was scarcely believable. Amid the pandemonium, a Swedish flag was found and along with the Brazilian flag was toted around the field by the victors, a thank-you to their hosts. At the awards presentation, though, it was the Brazilian flag which was hoisted highest because they were the champions.

As one element of the postgame celebration, the Brazilians were greeted on the field by King Gustav VI, the king of Sweden, who offered his own congratulations and presented the winning team with the trophy. It was the first time, but certainly not the last time that Pelé would come into contact with royalty or famous people through soccer. Also not imagined at that moment was that soon in his fantastic career, Pelé would be called "The King" also, as in the king of soccer. It was not a hereditary title, but an earned one.

"I've played in many worldwide games since then, but if I had to pick one great thrill," Pelé said years later, "it would have to be the 1958 World Cup. I still shiver when I recall the way people stood and applauded me after we won the championship game."[11]

You always remember your first time doing anything pleasurable and this was the first time Pelé was feted in such a huge display. Later in his career, it would become commonplace, but the young man who experienced these sensations at the time did not know if he would ever be in the same situation again.

Once the title was clinched and the players partied together, all Pelé wanted to do was get back to Brazil and share his joy with his family in Bauru. That wasn't going to be as simple as he thought it would be, however, because there were other obligations to fulfill. The rest of Brazil wanted to celebrate with its team, as well. What Pelé and his teammates probably knew instinctively, but not literally from their vantage point on the field, was that back home, after their triumph, their fellow countrymen took to the streets in major cities like Rio de Janeiro to dance the samba and party as a nation.

The range of jet planes was more limited in 1958 than they are now, so the long flight from Sweden to Brazil was made longer by the necessity to stop periodically and refuel. The first touch down inside Brazil was in Recife and it was there that the Brazilian players got their first taste of what their homeland thought of their victory. Just appearing at the airport on a stopover created a mob scene in Recife—the crowd snatched Vava and hoisted him upon burly men's shoulders and paraded him around. Then the people turned to other team members and treated them likewise.

In Rio, the reception was more tumultuous. When people realized their heroes had returned, they took to the streets again, singing, dancing, blocking traffic. Fireworks were set off. Rio is known for its annual Carnival, one of the great cultural touchstones of the country, but this was a spontaneous carnival and thousands upon thousands of citizens participated in the success and reveled in the triumph.

To an extent, the team was held hostage with love, transported from cocktail party to massive party, presented to government officials. Everyone wanted to laugh with the heroes, to touch the heroes, to hear what they had to say.

The best moment in Rio for Pelé was organized by the magazine *O Cruzeiro*, which brought the players' families to the city so they could also share in the festivities. Waiting for Pelé was his proud father, Dondinho, and his somewhat bemused mother, Dona Celeste, who had never believed in the power of soccer as a way to make a living, never mind make someone in her family nationally famous. All three of them shed tears. His mother tried to tell Pelé about the scope of the party held in Bauru when Brazil won the Cup.

"Our house was full," Dona Celeste said. "The street in front of the house was full. All the people who used to complain about you making too much noise, or breaking street lights, or being too fresh, or fighting all the time—even your school teachers—they all came to tell us how they always knew you would be a big success."[12] Apparently, Pelé had been granted a full neighborhood pardon for anything he ever did or ever thought of doing contrary to the rules.

Similar celebratory madness followed the team to Sao Paulo. Maybe it was even wilder there. Pelé described the team being "assaulted by the mob" at the airport and afforded uniformed protection. "It took hours to reach the center of the city from the airport," he said. "The crowds filled the streets and refused to budge, even for the big trucks that continually edged forward against them, horns blowing. Balconies on the sides of the streets were jammed with people throwing confetti, or torn newspaper, or dropping firecrackers. It was an insane asylum, run by the inmates."[13]

It was possible the victory celebration was more exhausting for the Brazilian players than the tournament had been. It was an astounding outpouring of affection and pride in what they accomplished. Every

Brazilian citizen would have loved to have been present in Sweden to witness the great victories first-hand, but that was not practical. Instead, they got to relive them second-hand, in a sense, once removed from the stadiums, but still with the players there, live and in person. The people and the players partied as if there was no tomorrow—which, given the nature of sport, was entirely possible. Just because Brazil won the 1958 World Cup did not mean it would win again in 1962—and that was so far in the future anyway, at the end of another four-year cycle. So why worry about it? The present was much more important.

Even after Sao Paulo, there was one last stop for Pelé, where he could soak up the adoration, where he was better known than he was anywhere else in the country. That was home in Bauru. Luncheons, dinners, parades, cocktail parties, luminaries shaking hands, Pelé thought he had seen it all during the drop-ins to Brazil's largest cities. This, Brazilian journalists sensed, was a big story. They understood Pelé had come from poverty, and that he left his home as a player with promise to join Santos less than two years earlier, and now he had become, virtually overnight, one of the most famous people in the country. This was to be his first time back in his hometown.

Pelé had no idea what to expect. His mother's description of the frenzy at her house and in the street in front of the house dropped hints, but that occurred in the moments after the team won. Time had passed. Surely people had gone back to their regular routines of work and school by now. Ah, but that was not the case. There was one last big bang of a celebration on Pelé's itinerary, and this one was just for him.

As the plane descended for its landing, Pelé could look out the window and see crowds on the ground. Police officers held the people back near the terminal. He admitted later that this sight provoked more excitement in him than similar and even larger scenes in Rio and Sao Paulo because this was his home.

"There was a big truck waiting for me, all ribbon and bunting, newly painted, it seemed, for the occasion," he said. "And standing before it was Sr. Nicola Avalone Junior, the major. " 'Bauru has been waiting for you, Pelé!' " is how he was welcomed.[14]

Pelé rolled through town in his truck, waving to his constituency like a beauty queen, the houses and buildings decked out in colorful banners. Old friends dashed up, jumped on the truck, and shook hands with him and said hello.

Finally, when the festivities ended and Pelé was dropped off at his parents' house, his excited brother, whose nickname was Zoca, informed him that the town was going to give him a car. Pelé laughed and said not to believe such rubbish because all sorts of gifts were supposedly being given to the team in the other cities, according to the newspapers, and none had materialized. Another reason Pelé did not believe the story was because cars were not so numerous in his poor community. They all had to be imported from the United States and the tax duty alone was horrendous. He calculated that it would cost about 55 years' worth of minimum wages, or more than the lifetime earnings of many people he knew, for them to afford to buy a car. A car as a gift? Ridiculous.

At a ceremony in Bauru, Pelé was presented with medals and trophies and plaques and hailed in speeches, and then, he really was presented with a car. It was not exactly the car of his dreams. The vehicle was called a Romisetta, it was tiny, and had only three wheels and no doors.

Pelé thanked all of the right people and the car was delivered to his home. He never used it, instead promptly gave it as a gift to his father. He explained that was the only thing that made sense because not only did he not have a driver's license and not know how to drive, but he also had no use for it in Santos because he was always traveling with the team. He forced the gift on his reluctant father.

At the time, Pelé still did not have the money to go out and buy himself a fancier car even if he wanted to do so. His salary was up to 6,000 cruzeiros a month for Santos, although he did receive a World Cup cash bonus.

Following his spectacular international debut in the World Cup and his return to Brazil as a soccer hero, it was obvious that soccer was going to be his profession and his home was going to be in Santos, or on the road, not in Bauru.

Pelé made a personal determination as he was turning from 17 to 18—he was now an adult.

NOTES

1. François Thebaud, *Pelé* (New York: Harper & Row Publishers, 1976), p. 14.

2. (No name), *Pelé* (West Haven, CT: Academic Industries, Inc., 1984), p. 37.

3. Pelé and Robert L. Fish, *My Life and the Beautiful Game* (New York: Doubleday & Company, 1977), p. 30.

4. Ibid.

5. Harry Harris, *Pelé: His Life and Times* (New York: Welcome Rain Publishers, 2001), p. 35.

6. Pelé and Fish, p. 38.

7. Harris, p. 44.

8. Pelé and Fish, p. 41.

9. Ibid., p. 46.

10. Harris, p. 47.

11. Bill Gutman, *Pelé* (New York: Grosset & Dunlap, 1976), p. 38.

12. Pelé and Fish, p. 58.

13. Ibid., p. 59.

14. Ibid., p. 61.

Chapter 3

THE BIGGEST STAR IN BRAZIL

The high of being World Cup champion passed and the country returned to normalcy. But Pelé's new normal was quite a bit different than it was before he left for Sweden. Santos, beginning to really appreciate what their young man brought to the field, promptly upped Pelé's salary to 13,000 cruzeiros a month. Soon after, Pelé's sort-of-contract expired and Santos rewarded him with a new deal for 15,000 cruzeiros a month, plus bonuses for games the team won.

Although the World Cup is played just once every four years (and soccer was part of the Summer Olympics, also on a four-year cycle, but two years apart from the World Cup), a club team such as Santos could stay very busy, not only in its own league, but by challenging top clubs from around the country and in other countries. Once Santos officials realized that Pelé was a top drawing card no matter where they might play, they redoubled efforts to schedule alluring contests against other clubs at home and also on the road (though they claimed a share of those profits, too).

Pelé was still young, only 19 at the end of October in 1959, and he was healthy and stronger, having grown into his body more, adding muscle and power. He was in fantastic shape and did not tire easily. As someone who, by the sport's general standards, was still a fairly raw player, what Pelé needed most to advance his game was more experience. Santos provided it with the club's ambitious schedule and it did not take long for Pelé to perfect his skills and gain the savvy adaptability necessary to deal with anything any team threw at him.

In 1959, Pelé scored 127 goals. The amount was so astonishing that his reputation soared throughout the continent and the world. It was as if Willie Mays or Mickey Mantle hit 80 or 90 home runs. Fans would say that was impossible. "Impossible" was the reaction of most soccer fans when they read of Pelé's feat. Impossible was also the word applied to moves that he made on the field when fans saw him for the first time.

Perhaps Pelé's most famous goal-scoring move that he adopted and developed during this period was the bicycle kick. It became his signature play, so brazen and difficult to execute that it never failed to astonish fans lucky enough to see him perform the shot in a game. Pelé did not invent the bicycle kick any more than Babe Ruth invented the home run. However, Pelé is identified with the shot the way Ruth is identified with the home run.

What makes the bicycle kick so attractive to watch is its innate difficulty and what seems to be the twisting of the body into a disadvantageous position for an attempt to goal. The player trying to complete the bicycle kick shot is parallel to the ground, in the air, rather than assuming a more customary position of kicking the ball with one foot and with the other foot firmly anchored.

"The kick is executed by throwing your body in the air, horizontally, with the shooting leg bent at the knee," Pelé said. "Then, just as the ball approaches, this leg is straightened up to propel the ball backward over the head. The hands are spread to cushion the fall."[1] In short, the proper form for the shot is even preposterous, never mind the athleticism called for to carry it out.

Pelé said that over the years, soccer fans have attributed the invention of the shot to him, but he declines parentage. It is his belief that the shot originated with a different Brazilian star named Leonidas, who represented the country in World Cup play in the 1930s and was a teammate of Waldemar de Brito, Pelé's one-time coach.

While many players dream of turning the acrobatic shot into a goal, not many even attempt it. It takes tremendous skill and body control to position oneself just right to have a chance to convert. On the periodic occasions when fans witness the bicycle kick, it leaves them delirious. It is rarer to see than a slam dunk on an alley-oop pass in basketball that shatters the backboard.

Pelé said that unlike many other players who find the bicycle kick a daunting challenge, it came easy to him, even as a youngster, and it was one thing that gave him confidence and the belief that he could become a better player than others.

"The other kids found it more difficult," he said, "and so already it was things like that that set me apart. It's a very Brazilian move and I am part of that."[2] Much later, when Pelé was rich and famous and signed endorsement deals, his picture on his own credit card showed him taking a bicycle kick.

By the end of July 1958, Pelé had scored 100 goals in his career. Less than a year later, he scored his milestone 200th goal. Although his base salary was not terribly impressive, Pelé and Santos won so many games, his bank account swelled from victory bonuses.

At all times during his tenure with Santos, the club sought to be a moneymaking operation, and having Pelé on the roster was an asset that could be milked for profitability. Although he was under contract, contracts expire, and once free of a deal, Pelé could make his own deal with a new team. Also, as an international sport, clubs from other countries could make bids for Pelé's services. Even when he was wedded to Santos, other teams could seek to buy him. There was no indication that Santos had any desire to sell Pelé, but that didn't stop clubs from making offers. In international soccer, the phrase used for buying and selling is a "transfer fee." It is the same thing, though. In the late 1950s, the record transfer fee—or purchase price—for a player was $100,000.

As Pelé scorched the nets game after game, winning favor and applause wherever he traveled, becoming an unstoppable offensive force, a rumor surfaced that Santos was being offered $1 million to sell Pelé to a team, or consortium of teams, or a league, in Italy. Brazilian fans at large were not particularly concerned if Pelé's contract was sold to another Brazilian club (they only wished it would be their favorite), but a feeling of unease, a real sense of worry, arose. What if Pelé was sold to a foreign team? That would be terrible.

The governing body of international soccer is known as FIFA, which stands for Fédération Internationale de Football Association. FIFA establishes rules for World Cup play and international play in general. Some residents of Brazil feared that if Pelé was transferred to a team in a different nation, he would—some day in the future—play against Brazil, not for Brazil. Although it may not have been generally known to the public, the rules did prevent that, however.

Then, a truly remarkable thing happened. The Brazilian government met and considered probably one of the most unusual pieces of legislation it had ever discussed. The legislators approved a bill to make Pelé "a national asset, a national treasure."[3] It was both a stunning compliment and a somewhat bizarre action. The action virtually labeled Pelé an inanimate commodity rather than treating him as a human being.

This meant that Santos was prevented from selling Pelé's soccer services to a club located in another country. That was essentially fine with Santos, which had not really been tempted to make such a deal, and it was basically okay with Pelé too, because he wanted to stay in Brazil.

For that matter, Pelé did not have any strong desire to depart from Santos and play for another Brazilian club. He felt a sense of loyalty to Santos for giving him his first big break; he liked his teammates, and as long as he was fairly compensated, he did not wish to join another team in the country.

The population of Santos swelled past 400,000 in the 2000s, though it was smaller when Pelé first went to live there. However, its seaside location and famed beachfront gardens adjacent to the Atlantic Ocean have long been alluring characteristics of the community. When Pelé joined Santos in the late 1950s, it was the first time in his life he had seen the ocean. In his mind, it was a fine place to live in, to be based in. The major city of Sao Paulo is less than 50 miles away.

Pelé had no itch to move on and to make sure he didn't change his mind, Santos grew ever-more generous in its contract dealings. In 1960, Pelé made 80,000 cruzeiros a month and was also granted a 60,000-cruzeiros living allowance. Bonuses from winning games reached 1 million cruizeiros that year. There were also perks as sidebars in the contract. Pelé was paid a signing fee which amounted to about $27,000, his mother was given a $10,000 house, and his father was given a new car. Apparently, by then, the midget automobile Pelé had presented to Dondiho was obsolete, but this was no Cadillac, either. It was a Volkswagen. Not that you would hear Pelé's father complain about that. It was payback time for his family, at last ridding his closest relatives of financial hardship. This was also genuine proof to Dona Celeste once and for all that if a player was talented and stayed healthy, he could indeed make a good living out of participating in the sport of soccer.

Pelé was learning that rather quickly, too. He was living up to the reputation he established in the World Cup. As great as winning the championship was, it was only the kicking-off point for his career, not a culmination. In 1960, Pelé scored 78 goals—a lower amount than the year before—but reflecting the fact that other teams treated him as a target, double-teaming his every move. Pelé passed more often to open teammates and Santos kept right on winning.

The next year, 1961, Pelé scored 110 goals. The man never slacked off. He was a miracle kicker, able to elude tight coverage, and score the big goals when his club needed them. It was clear that Pelé had not let his early success spoil him. He just got better and better, gradually becoming recognized as the best soccer player in the world.

Santos made sure that Pelé had a limited amount of free time during the season, and the more famous he became, off-season commitments and pursuits made sure he was equally busy when off the field. For relaxation, Pelé enjoyed fishing, and he had it in his financial power to rent a boat and go off to sea. In an era before cell phones and before major technological advances with personal computers, Pelé thought he could remove himself from the hubbub of everyday life this way, too. Sometimes, that escape plan wasn't good enough. Newspaper reporters actually chartered their own boats to chase him down at sea for conversations.

While it is far more difficult for a famous person to remain anonymous these days, with paparazzi photographers shadowing them and almost everyone carrying cell phones with cameras, Pelé's visage was so well-known in Brazil that he was ahead of his time, being forced to live a public life more than a half century ago, when that applied to only a tiny percentage of film stars and athletes.

Yet, in one very clever way, Pelé outfoxed reporters and gossip mongers who, given the teeniest chance, would have outed him about his relationship with his girlfriend. In the immediate period after Pelé's triumphant return from the 1958 World Cup and over the next couple of years, he quietly, even secretly, courted a young woman whom he had first met while watching a girls' club basketball game.

One day, Pelé and some teammates were killing time leading up to a big match against the Corinthians club and had been sequestered at a hotel. Bored and craving entertainment, but finding a limited supply, they showed up in the stands of a game, barely aware of who was playing.

Right away, Pelé, with his exceptional vision, focused on a back-up player on the bench for Corinthians. He kept his eye on her, and at one time, their eyes met. Pelé kept staring at her. When there was a break, some of the players came over to the Santos players and began mingling. The girl suddenly appeared at Pelé's side and they exchanged hellos. She recognized him and jauntily said, "Don't beat Corinthians too badly tomorrow."

That was Pelé's first conversation with the woman who would become his wife, Rosemeri, or Rose as he more frequently called her. "And with that, off she went, back to the reserves bench where she had been sitting," Pelé said. "I kept watching her, looking at her lovely brown hair, thinking what a beautiful girl she was. Even my teammates noticed that I'd been smitten. She'd made quite an impression on me."[4]

The next day, during his soccer game, Pelé kept scanning the stands for Rosemeri, but she did not attend. It wasn't until later that he found out she was only 14 years old (he was only 17 at the time) and still later before he discovered that she was from Santos, not Sao Paulo, as he believed. Pelé bumped into some of the girls from the basketball team on the street at home and was informed that Rosemeri worked in a nearby record store. Although he was not terribly caught up in the music scene, he did begin to make regular treks to the shop.

Their first talk at the store went well and Pelé asked if he could see Rosemeri again. She said she was too young to date, but if he wanted, he could visit her at home on a Saturday. The first Saturday that he could manage to do so, Pelé said he dressed up in his finest clothes and went to see Rosemeri. He was the first boy who had ever called on her and, as he pointed out, the first black boy who began wooing this white girl. However, there was never an issue about race in their relationship and on the first day, when they were just getting to know one another, Rosemeri's mother baked biscuits for them to eat.

Pelé may have been precocious about soccer and his career in that realm was rushed along at a swift pace, but nothing about his relationship with Rosemeri went fast. It was obvious to everyone involved, from Pelé to Rosemeri, and to her family, that any hint of their dating that seeped out from the knowledge held by a small group of people would blow up in the newspapers and become embarrassing. No one wished for that to happen, so for years, they kept it a group secret. Even for patient boys and girls, simply meeting and talking at the house was hardly enough entertainment. A cloak-and-dagger plan was hatched for visits to such events as the movies.

Going to movie theaters offered cover because it was dark inside. Rosemeri would go to the theater with one of her aunts and after the lights went down, Pelé bought his ticket and moved over to sit with them. This type of subterfuge went on for years and their relationship blossomed in secret. Never once did the press get a whiff of their dating.

Pelé was not one to care about skin color. There were white and black Brazilians on the national team and on his other teams. Rosmeri's parents appeared to be color blind, but Pelé was aware that was not always the case in daily life in Brazil despite its multiracial composition. When he was older, looking back at his life, Pelé said that he almost never encountered racial discrimination.

In my country the black race is not equal to the white race," Pelé said, "but nearly so." Jacques Lambert, a French professor regarded as an expert on Brazilian affairs, added, "Color is certainly a blemish in Brazil but it is not an irreparable blemish. Being black is not a defect impossible to overcome."[5] Brazil has long been a mixed-race nation.

That did not mean Pelé was unaware that some discriminatory feelings did exist. Once, he and two other black Santos players were late to a dinner because the last taxi from their location broke down and they did not hitchhike because they felt no one would give "three black boys" a ride, Pelé said. Upon more reflection, Pelé did recall an incident of huge embarrassment when he was 12 or 13, and he and a white girl in his class were getting close. They held hands and took walks. Then, one day, her father showed up at the school and in a rage, grabbed her by the arm and made her face Pelé. While the man berated her for spending time with this "black vagabond," writing notes to "this black tramp," and added that he did not raise his daughter to be seen "with trash like this," it was clear he was equally addressing Pelé. At the moment of the incident, Pelé was shocked into inaction, but soon wished he had battered the man to the ground with his fists. It would be incorrect to say that the incident scarred him, but he never forgot it.[6]

While Brazil had been an independent country for a long time, it had been a Portuguese colony, and there may well have been some vestiges of that sense of superiority still ingrained in white people. Some historians and sociologists have indicated a belief that it was victory in the 1958 World Cup championship game that propelled Brazil into a new era. Soccer was more than a national game, more a national institution. The parties and celebrations were so grand when Brazil bested Sweden for the crown because soccer meant so much to the people. Brazil may have become world champion in volleyball, and everyone would have thought that was nice, but they wouldn't have temporarily lost their minds over it. "The fact that the only unquestionable Brazilian hero is black constitutes a social phenomenon of the greatest importance," a French author noted after studying the nation and soccer in Brazil. "It is entirely correct, first, that the passion of Brazilians for 'futebol' is shared by all classes of society. In Brazil, futebol is the sport and on Copacabana beach as on the pebbly fields along Flamengo Bay, youngsters and adults come down . . . and face each other in mixed teams in daily matches."[7]

By 1961, Pelé was 21 years old, fully an adult. He really was his own man now. But he was a man with a conscience. For someone raised in poverty, it would have been easy and understandable for him to reach for every dollar he could to make up for the times of deprivation. He did not choose that route. If Pelé wished to make a higher salary, he could have engineered his sale to another, richer club than Santos. He stuck with the team that introduced him to the highest level of the sport. He was offered endorsement contract after endorsement deal to lend his name to more products than he had ever known existed while growing up in Bauru.

While Pelé was not shy about accepting endorsement money and slapping his name on commercials touting them, he drew a line. He would never accept deals with tobacco or liquor companies. With so much fame and money coming his way, it would have been easy for him to make a misstep, to tarnish his image, but while he had some advisors, innately, Pelé, who had been raised by religious, supportive, and honest parents, comprehended that his name was a precious commodity and that it was important that he keep his name clean. As the years passed and greater fame and riches flowed in his direction, he was even more careful and protective of the unique name, Pelé.

At heart a kind man, Pelé made many appearances for charities, and was especially easy to sign up for events that benefited children. It was commonly known, but not always publicized, that if children were in need, he would be there. He frequently visited Brazilian hospitals to cheer up kids who were sick. "I always have time for children," Pelé said, and it was a motto he lived by.[8]

Game after game, season after season, in those first three years back with Santos after the World Cup, Pelé left fans with their jaws slack as he twisted and contorted his body in ways that they did not believe possible as his goal count mounted. While he was not by nature boastful and did not provide what coaches refer to as bulletin-board fodder by making rash statements before Santos played against other teams, Pelé's mere presence on the field was an accidental form of arrogance. He was so sensational that when he showed up for a contest, the other team knew that Pelé would score a goal. The likelihood was almost a certainty, especially during his early prime years. Officially, Pelé averaged a goal per game for his entire career spanning around 20 years. At times, it seems as if defensively-oriented soccer teams don't average a goal per game, never mind a single player.

Some teams adopted the notion that no matter what happened, they would not allow Pelé to beat them. Yet, while Pelé's extraordinary vision and instincts generally paid off with a goal at least once during a 90-minute game, he was not a goal hog. He wanted the team to win, and if he was surrounded with no space to create a shot, he was content to feed open teammates. For that is what often happened when another squad drew up some fancy plan aimed at stifling him. That typically meant that another Santos player was uncovered and rather than succumb to the double team with a forced shot, Pelé might purposely draw the defenders to him and sneak a pass to his open teammate. Chances were that player would finish the play with a goal. The result was the same, even if the goal did not have Pelé's authorship of it.

Hoping for some insight from an impeccable source, a sportswriter once asked Pelé's own Santos coach, Antonio Fernandez, how he would design a defense to shut down his star. "I would put one man in back of him," Fernandez said, "and two men in front of him, all with guns. But I still don't think that would stop him once he got going towards the goal. Pelé is the best there ever was. They threw the mold away after they made him. He's a great inspiration, not only to the young players, but to the old players themselves."[9]

This was how the legend of Pelé grew. Acknowledged experts praised him in such effusive terms (even if Fernandez was a biased source as his coach) that the words seeped into the brains of the most casual fans. Pelé, Pelé, Pelé, they heard the name so often in the soccer world, starting with his auspicious World Cup debut in 1958, through his overwhelming goal-scoring exploits leading the nation's teams in that discipline season after season, they had to believe he was special.

It did not take long, though, for Pelé to morph from a young phenomenon to an established star, into a player described as being "the best there ever was." In 1962, when the World Cup was back after its four-year absence, and it was time for Brazil to defend the Jules Rimet Trophy, Pelé was no longer a bit player, a controversial selection for the team as a little-known up-and-comer. He was expected to be the leader of a team fully capable of winning the championship once again.

So little time had passed, but so much had happened to the boy become a man. Now, there was pressure on his shoulders. At the time of the 1962 World Cup, Pelé was still just 21 years old.

NOTES

1. Pelé and Robert L. Fish, *My Life and the Beautiful Game* (New York: Doubleday & Company, 1977), p. 99.

2. Pelé, *My Life in Pictures* (New York: Simon & Schuster, 2008), p. 16.

3. Joe Marcus, *The World of Pelé* (New York: Mason/Charter, 1976), p. 35.

4. Pelé, p. 36.

5. François Thebaud, *Pelé* (New York: Harper & Row Publishers, 1976), pp. 104–105.

6. Pelé and Fish, pp. 103–104.

7. Thebaud, pp. 103–104.

8. Marcus, p. 78.

9. Ibid., p. 82.

Chapter 4

WORLD CUP 1962

It is often said that the most difficult thing to accomplish in sports is repeating a championship drive. If that is true about teams that contend for titles each year, then that aphorism can be multiplied tenfold if the championship is sought on a four-year cycle.

The passage of four years with a team essentially marks a change of generations of players. Those who were older when the first title was won may have retired. Those who were younger would have matured. One thing that is often different is the expectations of the fans. In 1958, Brazilian fans were hopeful that the national team could capture the World Cup. In 1962, Brazilian fans acted almost as if they should win the World Cup again because it was their birthright. Brazil was the favorite, but no one among the players believed it would be an easy ride.

As for Pelé, his personal circumstances had changed dramatically between 1958 and 1962. If his knee injury had kept him out of the 1952 games, Brazilian fans would have noticed it, but barely missed him. In their minds, he was a 17-year-old boy along for the ride. It was not until Pelé took to the pitch and demonstrated his rare abilities on the world stage that they realized how important he was to the team.

In the intervening years, Pelé had indisputably become the biggest
name in the sport and the best player in the country, and maybe in
the world (the jury was still out at this point about him being the best
ever except in his coach's commentary). Now, Brazil was supposed to
win, Pelé was the leader, and he was supposed to carry his teammates
to victory. He had had four years to grow into the role of leader and he
embraced it, not shirked it, so he was ready for anything asked of him
by his coach, the fans, and his fellow players.

Back in 1958, Pelé was home in Bauru listening to the radio to
discover if he had been selected to compete for the national team.
In 1962, the question was who would be his teammates. Actually,
the core of the championship team did remain the same, with Pelé
aided and abetted by Garrincha, Vava, Didi, and other names familiar to Brazilian fans. While much of the team's administrative staff
also stayed the same, there was a new head coach. Vicente Feola did
not continue in his leadership role because he was ill. The new coach
was Aimore Moreira. There was soccer in the new man's blood. His
older brother, Zeze Moreira, coached the 1954 Brazilian World Cup
squad.

FIFA's 1962 World Cup was held in Chile, a much shorter trip for
the Brazilians, and they were placed in a group with Spain, Mexico,
and Czechoslovakia. Once again, however, Pelé was bothered by a
nagging injury, this time to his groin muscle. Pelé felt the strain was
brought on by playing too often and resting not enough, but unlike his
knee injury of 1958, he did not immediately consult with the training
staff and undergo its care, but kept quiet. "As in 1958, it looked like an
injury might dictate how many games I played," Pelé said. "But for now
I kept my anxieties to myself." [1]

Pelé was fine during the first game against Mexico, although Brazil
had a tougher time than expected and had to adjust its defensive formation in the second half to smother Mexico's chances on the way to a
2–0 victory. Pelé, and his partner, Zagallo, scored the goals. Pelé's was a
highlight film score, worth watching over and over again on tape.

"It was a goal I really enjoyed," Pelé said, "taking the ball past four
defenders before beating the great Mexican keeper, Carbajal, with a
powerful shot. The first game may have been safely negotiated, but
I was in trouble. I walked off the pitch feeling unusually tired, really

Pelé in 1962 as he looked when he first established himself as the greatest soccer player in the world—and was on his way to establishing himself as the greatest soccer player of all time. (AP Photo)

weary in my bones, and I knew I had to go and see (team physician) Dr. Hilton Gosling. He made me promise to keep him informed about how I felt, and I did, but I was terrified he'd put me on the bench and so I kept the real extent of my worries to myself."[2]

That was probably a mistake. Professional athletes often assume a warrior's mentality and have a belief in their own invulnerability. They are more shocked than observers when their bodies fail them. Sometimes they need another party's opinion on whether or not to take a rest because left to their own judgment they might never step back, the main reason being exactly what Pelé feared—a medical professional might ground them, take the car keys away like a parent, and force them to rest.

In Pelé's case, it may already have been too late. He wasn't going to sit out if he could walk and his body was on the verge of breaking down, as if it was a rubber band stretched too tight. In the next game, against Czechoslovakia, Pelé began one of his patented runs to the goal. He faked out defenders, wound up, and booted a hard shot at the net. As he did so, the muscle in his groin gave way and Pelé fell to the ground as if he had been shot. Although from a treatment standpoint it was unwise for Pelé to continue, under FIFA rules, there could be no substitute. The choice was to play with just 10 men against the Czechs' 11, or have Pelé hobble through the rest of the game. He chose the latter and stayed in the game. Afterward, Pelé thanked the Czech defenders for their sportsmanship. The opposing players did not take unnecessary runs at Pelé, who was the proverbial sitting duck unable to protect himself from tackles. The game ended 0–0.

It had now gone too far for Pelé to mask his injury and Dr. Gosling ruled him out for the next game against Spain. Ironically, as Pelé was forced to the sidelines, a newcomer named Amarildo was activated to take his place in the lineup and scored both goals in the 2–1 win. Pelé had the passing thought that maybe Amarildo would take advantage of his absence and become the new Pelé. He had not yet come to realize that there never would be a new Pelé, that he was the one and only. Good health is always the most important thing in life because without it, depression often follows and the mind is clouded. "As I lay in bed I couldn't help but wonder if possibly Pelé was all through at the age of 21," Pelé pondered, "and if Amarildo would be the next Pelé. He had certainly played as brilliantly as Pelé, or anyone else in that game, and deserved all the credit he received. All finished at 21! I gritted my teeth and told Mario Americo to make the towels hotter." [3]

Whether the fear of becoming a young has-been was realistic or not, Pelé used the thought as a motivator. After the triumph over Spain gave Brazil two wins and a tie in its group, the squad moved on to the quarterfinals. The opposition was England. England was one of the great soccer-playing nations, the home of where the game began and where the modern rules were established in 1863. As in Brazil, soccer was the national sport of England, the one fans were most passionate about and indeed followed with fanaticism. There was great respect between the two sides, with an awareness of how talented each team was, and the history of meetings between Brazil and England was characterized by their importance.

England had been in a bit of a slump internationally, but in 1962, the program was again on the rise, infused with new blood. One of team's new stars was Bobby Moore, a player who would soon lead his country to great glory. Pelé very much wanted to play against England, especially since the opposition was a serious threat to Brazil advancing. But his leg was not well enough to take the pounding in a 90-minute game, and again, he was benched. Brazil prevailed 3–1, and Garrincha orchestrated the offense with Pelé's usual sharpness.

Brazil moved on to the semifinals where the defending champions met the tournament hosts. The pain had subsided in Pelé's leg, but he had not tested the muscle, and once again Dr. Gosling said "no way" to him playing. The team again rose to the moment without Pelé and defeated Chile 4–2, with Garrincha and Vava scoring two goals each. Pelé was incredibly frustrated over his inaction and with the final looming against Czechoslovakia, he was determined to get back into the lineup. Enough was enough. He had to play in the World Cup final.

Pelé hauled his body out to the practice field. The pain had disappeared, so he began working out with the most rudimentary of plays. He began by taking corner kicks. On the very first kick, he felt a shooting pain. He was done. Pelé was going to miss competing in the championship game and he broke down crying at his plight. He sat out the final as Brazil won without him by a 3–1 margin. "It's difficult to describe the devastation I felt, the disillusionment," he said. "I cried so much, and not just because I was in agony. It seemed so unfair, after turning up to games day in, day out for my club, army and country, here I was sidelined before the second biggest game of my life."[4]

In the United States, where soccer was played, but not at the level it was practiced in Europe or South America, coverage was provided by *Sports Illustrated*. It may have been the first time the average American sports fan heard of Pelé, referred to as "The Black Pearl" in the magazine's story. Unfortunately, this introduction came by way of reports on his injury. "There are two Brazilian teams," said Alberto Cassoria, president of the Chilean Football Coaches Association. "One with Pelé, one without. They do not resemble each other at all. The second one may not be good enough to win."[5] The writer was forced to find perspective from a viewer like Cassoria, one step removed from the action because none of the 16 coaches were talking to sportswriters prior to their games and they all forbade players from indulging in such interviews either.

Eventually, when the writer gained an audience with Moreira, the Brazilian coach, and it was suggested that Pelé was maybe a little bit like Willie Mays, the coach said, "Willie who?" The writer was trying to draw the coach out on the parallels between the great baseball star, who could beat an opposing team any number of ways, and the athletically brilliant Pelé, who could do the same. Whether he realized it or not, in the rest of the world, any comparison would have been reversed. It was also true enough that the same writer approaching a Major League baseball team manager with a similar question might have received the answer, "Pelé who?"[6]

As happy as the next Brazilian that the squad defended its championship, it was not the same joyous return. He was part of the celebration this time, but not the focus of it, and for him, at least, it was more muted. Disappointed by his injury, Pelé was out of commission for two more months.

When Pelé returned to action, it was for Santos, and healed and rested, he continued to play terrific soccer with a fresh fierceness. There was no way to make up for missing the World Cup games (thankfully, the team won anyway, he felt), but whatever the next highest level title he could compete for, Pelé wanted to make sure Santos won it. That is what happened next. He led Santos to the South American Club Championship and also led Brazil in scoring for the fifth straight year. One thing Pelé proved was that he was still as good as ever, maybe better, and that what he considered a personal letdown in the World Cup was beyond his control, but not a problem that would be ongoing. And although he was only to play a shortened schedule in the World Cup, Pelé was still voted Brazil's player of the year by sportswriters.

Among the most famous "futebol" clubs in the world in the 2000s are Manchester United and Real Madrid. But when Pelé was a member of Santos, that club held an international distinction and beyond accounting for domestic obligations, Santos' management was all for touring the world and taking on the best any nation had to offer. Their not-so-secret weapon was Pelé. He was both a thrilling player who gave his team an edge and also a drawing card for the fans of the world. Santos signed deals to play teams anywhere and everywhere and the club piled up more flying miles than foreign diplomats. The early 1960s was an era before airline frequent flyer miles were awarded, but if they had been available, Pelé and his teammates would have been members of million-mile clubs and able to obtain tickets to fly free anywhere from Istanbul to Calgary.

While Pelé's base salary was comparatively modest for such a big star, his interests coincided with Santos' interests on the business side, as well as the scoreboard. Pelé accrued bonuses not just for showing up, but for winning. The more Santos won, the richer Pelé got. The absolute best athletes in the United States were reaching the $100,000 mark in some cases, but there were not many of them. Pelé surpassed all in earnings. Although the figure is murky before the mid-1960s, it was acknowledged that he was the best-compensated athlete in the world.

Concurrent with that were continuing rumors in the Brazilian press that foreign clubs were still after him. This was despite the government's declaration of him as a national treasure. The source of the rumors was unknown, but the alleged buyers were teams in Italy and Portugal. At one point, Pelé felt compelled to hold a press conference to announce—nothing. The point was to inform the soccer world and the Brazilian public that he was not going anywhere, that there was no deal, no sale, no Pelé moving to another land. Furthermore, Pelé informed the world that he would not be open to such offers in the future either. He was going to stay with Santos, now and forever, or at least as long as he played top-level international soccer. Period.

When he took that first train from Bauru to Santos, Pelé was an innocent lad. He was struck by the sight of the ocean for the first time. Within a few years, however, he had seen glimpses of all kinds of the world's geographic features from oceans to mountains, from farmland to major cities. Soccer was his passport and it opened his eyes to the world's diversity while at the same time reinforcing the sport as a common denominator everywhere. "We played at sea level one day and at 8,000 feet the next," Pelé said of travels with Santos. "We played before Indians wearing derby hats, Mexicans in sombreros, Dutch islanders with peaked caps."[7]

Despite the interruption of his steady ride because of injury in the 1962 World Cup tournament, by 1963 Pelé's wizardry had been examined, studied, and applauded not only throughout Brazil, but around the world, and the conclusion had been reached with certainty—he was the best soccer player in the world. Lula, his early coach, chimed in with his thoughts at that time. "Pelé can no longer be compared to anyone else," Lula said. "He is fast on the ground and in the air, he is strong, has a good shot, good ball control, an ability to control play, a feeling for the move, he is unselfish, good-natured and modest."[8] If Pelé ran for Pope, then Lula would be his campaign manager.

On the field, just when it seemed that Pelé could do nothing more to impress his public, a game would come along that once again left fans buzzing and those in the stadium congratulating themselves for being in attendance. In 1964, Pelé's goal-scoring total dipped to 60, attributable in his mind to the new defensive outlook teams were adopting. Maybe in their efforts to avoid humiliation because of his feet, Pelé's foes developed new stratagems, dropping back more and more players in their defensive alignments. For someone who was a goal scorer, Pelé thought such maneuvers translated to boring soccer. The people wanted goals and he provided them. Other teams sought to stay within comeback range of Santos, holding the club to 1–0 tallies. It saved face. A loss was still a loss, but it was less embarrassing to lose 1–0 or 2–1 than by 6–0. When Pelé was around and in top form, there was no telling when lightning would strike or an avalanche of goals would bury his opponents.

Such an occasion did break out in November of that year when Santos was on the road in Ribeirao for a game against the Botafogo club. It would be an historic day. In an 11–0 victory, Pelé scored eight goals and set up two others with assists. Witnesses said Pelé passed up two surefire goals and passed off or he might have scored 10 goals that day. In Pelé's mind, it was less of an achievement than a reflection that the opposition was weak, so he didn't wish to gloat over the accomplishment. "The first four or five goals were real fun," he said, "but the game was so one-sided that I didn't really think about the other three goals. I just wanted the game to end and when it did I was happy it was over. I really felt sorry for the other team's goalie. Our goalie had such an easy time of it he could just as easily have taken a chair and sat down waiting for them to come in and take a shot on him. Give me a close game anytime. That I enjoy."[9]

Despite that earth-moving performance, 1964 was not a great year for Pelé. He suffered three different nagging injuries that slowed him down, and though he was not overtly publicly irritated about the variety of defenses thrown his way, he thought it was bad for the sport overall. "Soccer today has become far too defensive," Pelé said. "It is no longer a show. This is bad for the public. There are many teams that do well not because they are good but because they are very negative. I don't enjoy a game in which the other team plays only defense. That doesn't allow the fans to see an exciting or even a well-played game." [10]

Friendly to all soccer fans wherever he traveled, Pelé always took time to sign autographs. He was cooperative with sportswriters when they wanted answers to their questions. He was loyal to his club and so revered, his own government wanted to put an electric fence around his playing opportunities to hem him into the nation's borders. So it was not terribly surprising that Pelé was approached and asked to run for public office. On name recognition alone, he might have won in a landslide. However, he wanted to have nothing to do with the political arena which he knew could get nasty. Although Pelé's refusals were polite, most likely he wanted to slam the door in the faces of the power brokers. He had not the slightest interest in becoming a politician. "I have always stayed out of politics and race relations," Pelé said. "I feel that I am doing what I do best and as far as race relations are concerned I respect everybody for what they are—not for their religion or the color of their skin. I want the people to judge me on the soccer field. I am a soccer player and that is what I am interested in. I think I always will feel the same way no matter what else I accomplish in my life." [11]

Pelé was a soccer player and he was going to stay a soccer player, even if some people made it seem that being the best in the world, playing a game was not a worthy enough pursuit. In its own way, soccer was a religion to many of the people and Pelé was a god of that religion.

NOTES

1. Pelé, *My Life in Pictures* (New York: Simon & Schuster, 2008), p. 39.

2. Ibid.

3. Pelé and Robert L. Fish, *My Life and the Beautiful Game* (New York: Doubleday & Company, 1977), p. 169.

4. Pelé, p. 41.

5. Roy Terrell, "Viva Vava and Garrincha!" *Sports Illustrated*, June 25, 1962.

6. Ibid.

7. Pelé and Fish, p. 150.

8. Harry Harris, *Pelé: His Life and Times* (New York: Welcome Rain Publishers, 2001), p. 66.

9. Joe Marcus, *The World of Pelé* (New York: Mason/Charter, 1976), p. 51.

10. Ibid.

11. Ibid., p. 53.

Chapter 5

MARRIAGE, PROBLEMS, AND SUPER FAME

Once Pelé set his eye on Rosemeri Cholby, he embarked on a quiet, long-term courtship that lasted years. For someone as often in the lime-light as he was, he did a remarkable job of keeping their relationship secret and hiding it from prying photographers.

He may have been so successful at this because likely the news-hounds of the time figured he would be busy dating prominent models, not a girl just entering high school. Since they were so discreet on the rare occasions they went out, Pelé and Rosemeri were also well-positioned to fool anyone who suspected Pelé of a serious romance and wanted to publicize it in a gossipy way.

Many of Pelé's visits with Rosemeri were routine stopovers at her house. As a teenager, when they rendezvoused in public places, she was always chaperoned, and they did not flaunt their time together in highly obvious ways either. They hid their connection from the media superbly, especially when Rosemeri was young and they pulled off the in-the-darkness movie tricks they had been accustomed to employing.

In this modern era of high technology, tweets, and camera phones, it would be much more difficult to remain anonymous in a prying society than it was a half-century ago, but even then, it took some subterfuge to pull off their out-of-the-house appearances without being noticed.

More and more, Pelé was a big shot who attracted newspaper, magazine, and television attention like a magnet, some of it going beyond the boundaries of the country. At first, he was merely a national hero, but the more frequently Pelé competed internationally, the more the soccer press around the world took note of his skills and accomplishments. Yet still, the all-around intrusiveness in the lives of the famous was a fraction of what it would be in the current day and age.

From the first moment Pelé laid eyes on Rosemeri at her basketball game, Pelé was indeed smitten. It was not a passing emotion either. He was determined to get to know her, determined to stick with her until she was more grown up, and he determined after a little while to make her his bride. As for Rosemeri, she may have recognized Pelé the first time she saw him in the stands at the basketball game because of his growing notoriety, but she was level-headed enough not to fall for him just because he was a star athlete. They very much took their time getting to know one another.

The Pelé–Rosemeri cloistered relationship lasted seven years. Periodically, Pelé would raise the subject of marriage and Rosemeri put him off, saying she was too young. Seven years was long enough for Pelé to wait. It was 1965 when he spoke frankly to Rosemeri and told her he was going to officially ask her father, Guilherme, for her hand in marriage the following weekend, when the two men had an appointment to go fishing. Even then, Rosemeri demurred, but not in a firm way this time. "I was pretty confident he would give us his blessing," Pelé said. "After all, I had shown my love for her in my patient wooing over the years and he knew I was making a good living and could provide for her."[1] After living with team members in a somewhat haphazard fashion as a bachelor for years, Pelé had obtained a new house as part of his latest contract with Santos. It was so large that he moved his immediate family in from Bauru and there was plenty more room for young newlyweds.

In their fishing boat the next weekend, Pelé waited until Rosemeri's father was in a good mood after catching his first fish of the day to inform him that he wished to take his daughter's hand in marriage. Pelé later speculated that Guilherme could not have been terribly surprised that the question came up. "After all, I had been eating his wife's cakes and cookies and drinking his soft drinks and milk for a good many years, and one has to wonder at such devotion to snacks," Pelé said. Pelé expected his prospective father-in-law to either hug him with joy or to vehemently reject the idea.[2]

He was a bit taken aback when Rosemeri's father did not immediately grant permission and bless them, or refuse him. Instead, Guilherme said the matter had to be taken up with Dona Idalina, Rosemeri's mother. When the issue was taken before her, she immediately approved and asked what had taken them so long.

When it leaked out that Pelé was going to marry, it caught many of the sportswriters who followed his career by surprise. They didn't even know he had a special someone. Pelé had eluded them much the way he eluded defensive players that tried to corner him as he brought the ball up-field. Pelé and Rosemeri had been surprisingly successful keeping their romance out of the gossip columns.

It was in February 1966, during Carnival Week, Brazil's biggest party, that Pelé and Rosemeri wed. The goal was to carry out the ceremony in privacy, but rumors spread, and Pelé and Rosemeri did not marry in complete secrecy. The couple actually had a small ceremony, basically surrounded by immediate family. However, if a Brazilian citizen was reading the newspapers that week, he might have thought there would be 100,000 people in attendance.

"There had been a lot of speculation in the press on the run-up to the wedding, most of it nonsense," Pelé said. "One report had it that we were going to be married by the Pope himself, another that we had invited so many people that we'd had to hire the Pacaembu Stadium as the venue for the ceremony. It was understandable that there was a lot of interest, but some of the attention went too far, and I was deeply offended by some articles expressing disapproval that I, a black man, was marrying a white woman."[3]

However, while those crass articles did exist and did offend, other publications wrote about Pelé and Rosemeri from the perspective that the interracial couple was a positive symbol of a nation that was color blind and that was more multiracial than most. After that, the skin color differences between Pelé and his spouse basically disappeared as a topic.

The wedding was actually conducted at Pelé's parents' old home in Santos with the local parish priest officiating. There was no way of keeping such a secret in the neighborhood, but it wasn't as if all of Sao Paulo or Rio was in on it. The privacy was maintained in the house for the ceremony. Outside, well, that was another matter. It was pretty crowded on the old street where young Pelé, now 25, once played with his friends.

"In the street beyond the wall, kept at bay by police, were mobs of people, all trying to get a glimpse of the bride, the groom, or anyone else who might have been a member of the small wedding party," Pelé said. "We had a small reception there in the house, and once the crowd got tired of hanging around and went on about the usual business of Carnival, Rose and I made our escape."[4]

It would have been virtually impossible to escape notice of the press if Pelé and Rosemeri conducted their honeymoon in Brazil. This was one time Pelé's fame as a soccer player paid dividends for him. Roland Endler, who was a rich man from Munich, was such a huge fan of Pelé's game that he often visited from Europe and traveled with Santos merely to watch Pelé play. He wanted to give the couple a grand present, but initially, Pelé refused. When, instead, Endler offered Pelé and his bride a trip to Europe, they accepted. During the rumor stages promulgated by the press in Brazil leading up to the wedding, one newspaper stated that the Pope would officiate the ceremony. That was erroneous, but when the couple visited Rome, they did have an audience with Pope Paul VI. Actually, in 1961, the religious Pelé and his Santos teammates had met Pope John XXIII.

Not long after they married, Pelé and Rosemeri started a family. The first child was a daughter, Kelly Cristina, born in 1967, and the second child was a boy, born in 1970 as Edson Cholby do Nascimento. Unlike the spouses of some celebrities who routinely appear on their arms in public, Rosemeri was a homebody. She did not enjoy the glare of attention that followed her husband and that he became used to dealing with wherever he went. For her, staying behind the scenes at home was perfectly fine. Pelé's family could afford anything it wanted or needed, and one thing Rosemeri did not feel she needed was to be photographed going to the grocery store or attending star-studded events with Pelé.

Pelé, his wife Rosemeri, and baby daughter, Kelly Christina in 1967. Pelé engaged in a very quiet courtship of Rosemeri over a long period of time to avoid media attention, but many years later, they split up and Pelé remarried. (AP Photo)

While it was not summarized by Pelé so succinctly until later years, when he was a true worldwide figure, he in many ways viewed himself as just another guy with a special talent. The Pelé that was beloved to the public was a confident, yet humble man, who did not consider himself as royalty elevated to that stature by the sport of soccer. It would not be long before Pelé actually became probably as famous throughout the universe as the pope. He may have had audiences with the pope and heads of nations, but he put on no airs.

"Kings, dictators, presidents of republics, governors, have always treated me with the greatest respect," Pelé said. "I have behaved in the same way toward them, the same way I behave with unknown spectators who come toward me in a stadium."[5] That could be described as the behavior of a holy man, but Pelé most definitely made no pretensions to being such a personage.

A wife, of course, is not going to put a husband on a pedestal the way an adoring public might. In this case, Rosemeri in her conversations with the soccer superstar who became her husband, called him Edson, not Pelé. It was as if, to her, Pelé was a stage name and Edson was the real man.

Pelé did not want a large merchandise gift from Endler, his supporter, but the escape route to Europe was enticing, and while it may not have been general knowledge, the richest athlete in the world in earnings was hurting for money because his chief advisor had let him down. Pelé had allowed his close friend Pepe Gordo to manage his money, and not long before Pelé's marriage, Gordo informed him that the money was gone. Somehow, it had been squandered, and Pelé was facing the prospect of bankruptcy.

This was overwhelming news. Pelé had lived in poverty as a boy and thought he had left it behind. It was quite sobering to hear that he may have lost his cushion, his insurance, his bank account to poor investments and that he teetered on the edge of insolvency. This was difficult to believe. Pelé was irate and disappointed, but also concerned as he embarked on a new life as a married man. He was still young, in his prime as a soccer player, and he was under contract to Santos for a considerable sum, so he did have a lifeline and earning power. But he was buried in a morass of paperwork and he faced not only the possibility of bankruptcy, but public humiliation. The newspapers would be all over this morsel and the public, his fans, would ask aloud how it was possible that the richest athlete in the world could go bankrupt. Pelé had worked hard to establish a reputation not only as a great soccer player, but a responsible member of society. He was no troublemaker, not a lawbreaker.

This was a dismaying situation. Pelé knew he had to extricate himself from the situation which was on the verge of degenerating into a potentially messy court case where he would be sued for payments that he could not make because of the financial losses suffered that he had not known about. Not knowing was one thing, but in the eyes of the law, he would be held accountable and his name would be trashed.

First, Pelé sought the advice of an expert who looked into his holdings and finances. He concluded that the circumstances may even have been worse than had been reported to him by Pepe Gordo. Pelé realized too late that he had given away too much power and believed too implicitly in his friend's capability. When the topic of using bankruptcy as a shield was suggested, Pelé was almost ready to vomit; he felt so dizzy and sick at the prospect. "I thought of the punishment I had taken on the football field, the target of kicks from every defender who wanted to be a hero to his fans and put me in a hospital," Pelé said. "I thought of playing those two 45-minute halves without a second's rest, running myself ragged, just to build for the future. The future? What future? It was all in some set of accountant's books I could not pretend to understand and it wasn't a future at all. It was a past, and a painful and expensive one at that."[6]

Pelé felt hemmed in by his situation. After much thought, he went to the board of directors of Santos and explained. His bosses agreed to cover his debts, but in return, asked for him to sign a new, three-year contract that was strict in its provisions. The first year would provide Pelé with his normal salary and finances. The second year, he would play for no increase. The third year, he would play for free. Seeing no other solution to his problem, he signed.

Pelé had learned a hard lesson and after this financial fiasco, he was a much more hands-on administrator of his money and his business deals. He did regain his footing and once again emerged as the highest paid and richest athlete in the world, but this was a disappointing blow and it was something he did not completely shake off.

On the one hand, Pelé had never been happier. He had at last married his sweetheart whom he had fallen in love with at first sight, his reputation was saved, and at the same time, his fame continued to spread. Santos continued to make its annual ambitious schedule and by appearing in and playing in so many countries, Pelé grew into a worldwide figure. Even in countries where soccer did not matter so much (the United States being the main one), Pelé became so well-known that he transcended the sport. When he met the pope, he was only warming up. As the short, one-word name became ingrained first in soccer fans' minds, and then in casual sports fans' minds, Pelé became so widely known that eventually it was conceded that he was the most famous person on the planet.

Pelé transcended sport. He transcended race. He transcended religion. He possessed a winning smile and a body, while muscular, with massively developed thighs so appropriate for use in soccer, but he was no physical giant. In looks, he was Everyman, and so Everyman identified with him. He was exceptionally popular at home in Brazil, naturally. He was wildly popular in Latin America by proximity and frequent appearances in games against other Latino countries. He was revered in countries where the black population was the majority. And he was marveled at in countries where the white population was dominant, but where soccer was the chief sport.

On the other hand, although he was known in the United States, he was not venerated there with the same passion. Perhaps that was due to his being a black man at a time when race relations in the United States were poor and African Americans were still fighting for their civil rights, sometimes through riots in the streets. There were numerous black American athletes that were admired for their skills, including such basketball stars as Bill Russell, Wilt Chamberlain, and Oscar Robertson, such baseball stars as Willie Mays, and such football stars as Jim Brown. They not have been beloved, but they were popular for their accomplishments. Still, it was likely that ignorance and lack of appreciation for big-time soccer counted more against Pelé than his skin color did in the United States. Compared to other nations around the world, soccer was considered a second-rate sport in the United States. It did not rise to the level of popularity of baseball, football, and basketball, or even hockey. In the late 1950s through the 1960s, soccer probably ranked behind boxing and track and field, and the Triple Crown horse races as well.

In an era when there was no Internet and the United States was more inwardly focused, except when it came to international intervention with its troops, the king of soccer was not going to cause pandemonium by walking through Times Square in New York City. That would have to wait.

Elsewhere, where soccer was one of the most universal of things closely followed in a country, Pelé's stature began to grow. One minute, it seemed, he was a star. Then, people were calling him the king of soccer. Eventually, he was looked at as a god. Pelé had a wife who knew he was just a man. He had teammates on Santos, his club team, and on the Brazilian national team, who recognized his great soccer ability, but did not inflate him in their minds as something beyond a human being. Yet, when they spent time with Pelé at stadiums, in the community, or on the road in other locales, they were sometimes thunderstruck at what they witnessed. "Some people wanted to touch him," teammate Clodoaldo said. "Some people wanted to kiss him. In some countries they kissed the ground he walked on. I thought it was beautiful, beautiful."[7]

Pelé made friends on the pitch because he played a highly skilled, but clean game. There was nothing opponents could do but stand in awe of him when they threw their toughest defenses at him, and yet, he was still able to dribble around and through them. Pelé was such a brilliant ball handler with his feet that on memorable occasions, he could maneuver around three or four converging defenders and still either fake out the net-minder or feed a perfect pass to a teammate who moved in unmolested for a shot.

Just Fontaine, a one-time French soccer star of an earlier generation, but a coach when Pelé was playing, could not have described a son in more glowing terms that those he applied to the Brazilian wizard. "If good fairies of soccer exist, they all got together around Pelé's cradle and showered him with gifts. This feline, this black panther, contains all the qualities that soccer demands. His speed, his jumping ability, his head play, his shooting, and his reading of the game are dazzling. He is unadulterated dash, the god of soccer who came down from Mount Olympus to preach on earth, the natural player, naturally endowed with the rarest of gifts." Fontaine gushed on and on, presumably pausing for breath at some point before issuing more superlatives. In the end, Fontaine said he could not remember Pelé making a single mistake at his position.[8]

Even Pelé would dispute that aw-shucks conclusion, but he had that brainwashing effect on people as his game only improved in his twenties. He showed no signs of slowing down, only signs of mastering every situation he faced.

NOTES

1. Pelé, *My Life in Pictures* (New York: Simon & Schuster, 2008), p. 45.

2. Pelé and Robert L. Fish, *My Life and the Beautiful Game* (New York: Doubleday & Company, 1977), p. 177.

3. Pelé, p. 45.

4. Pelé and Fish, p. 183.

5. François Thebaud, *Pelé* (New York: Harper & Row Publishers, 1976), p. 112.

6. Harry Harris, *Pelé: His Life and Times* (New York: Welcome Rain Publishers, 2001), pp. 71–72.

7. Ibid., p. 66.

8. Thebaud, pp. 162–163.

Chapter 6

WORLD CUP 1966

Four years is a long time to wait for another championship, but Brazilian fans were on top of the world and they strongly believed that their guys could capture a third straight World Cup title in 1966. If they did so, they would retire the Jules Rimet Trophy to Brazil. Rather than gaining temporary possession for four years, the country would gain permanent possession for display and Cup officials would introduce a new trophy.

So many things change with coaches and personnel as the seasons pass that teams are always in flux from one World Cup to another. Brazil was playing the best and most colorful, offensively-oriented soccer in the world and Brazil featured the best player in the world in Pelé, but that did not mean, even after two consecutive triumphs, that during the month's length of play in the 1966 World Cup, Brazil would again have the best team.

The achievement of collecting a championship is a dream come true in any sport. Sustained excellence is another matter altogether. Stability and continuity spread over years as the World Cup cycle demanded was a greater challenge yet. Brazilian soccer fans had reached the point where they took victory for granted and Pelé's exploits as a given. To them, it seemed inconceivable that the Brazilian national team could be vulnerable after sweeping to two straight World Cup titles.

Above all, Brazil had Pelé and no one else had Pelé. The teenager who had made the 1958 World Cup his coming-out party was now fully grown and fully formed, and while slight compared to gladiators in certain other sports, he was five feet, eight inches and weighed about 165 pounds. Much of that was muscle. In the eight intervening years between the World Cup of 1958 and the World Cup of 1966, much had changed for Brazil and Pelé. Brazil was regarded as the best outfit in the world, although now it was time to prove it again, and Pelé was regarded as the best player in the world—something he proved almost every day. He wished nothing more than to lead his country to victory again at the upcoming World Cup, but as the days dwindled to departure time for Europe, he had misgivings.

Pelé spotted problems on the horizon very early in the process. He was very uneasy over things that he saw in the making and shaping of the team, in some of the behind-the-scenes operations that fans never see, are never aware of, or don't consider consequential.

Looking at the written record of the history of Brazilian soccer even now, avid fans would like to pretend 1966 never happened. Brazil put its stamp on world soccer in 1958 and 1962. Brazil carried forward and rejuvenated its status after 1966. But 1966—that was one World Cup that Brazil, in retrospect, should have been perfectly content to sit out, to avoid even showing up in England. Beforehand, though, Brazil was giddy with expectation, bulging with such pride from the previous conquests that perhaps a bit of focus was lost in preparing for another Cup try. Pelé certainly thought that was the case.

"We were thinking about the possibilities of being thrice champions now," he said. "The whole country was buzzing with the possibility. There was not a soul who was not touched by this exaggerated optimism. As far as the directors were concerned we were just going over there to fetch the Cup, take it around, show the other countries, and then bring it home. Everyone thought we'd win with ease. But our preparations were not planned with the same humility as in 1958 or 1962. We were already starting to lose the title before we set foot in England."[1]

From the start of training camp, Pelé was skeptical about some procedures being followed. He thought the list of invitees—40 strong—

was too large and inhibited the crispness of practices. Many top players from the previous squads had retired and he wondered if the men who were going to replace them had the same level of talent. Pelé disagreed with the idea of splitting the hopefuls into four teams and stationing them all over the country rather than in one central location. The logistics between the groups was poor.

When the team embarked for Europe, it was less a unit than a collection of players and when competition began, that showed. Pelé described Brazil's performance this way: "Total, shameful failure."[2] Even before the real competition began in England, there were signs of weakness in games against other European teams. As warm-ups to sharpen their game, the Brazilians played clubs in Spain, Scotland, and Sweden. Pelé thought the scheduling was silly. There didn't need to be so many exhibition games in so many different places so close to the meaningful tournament.

This late in the process, it seemed as if Brazil was trying to rebuild on the fly. One by one, veterans of Cup-winning teams were cut from the final roster even as they played well. Pelé and the remaining confidantes were astounded.

"As a result the players lost confidence in the Technical Commission, if they ever had any, as well as confidence in themselves as a team," Pelé said. "The directors, on the other hand, were still so blithely sure that Brazil was going to walk away with the trophy that they spent little time worrying about exactly which eleven men they were going to field for any game." A team meeting was called, the bosses told the players not to worry, they were doing fine, and surely they would win their five Cup games and claim the trophy once more. To Pelé, it seemed the directors had no inkling of a problem. He said when he walked out of the meeting with compatriot Garrincha that if he had been a drinking man, he would have gone drinking.

Brazil opened with Bulgaria, a weaker team, and won 2–0. Pelé was disappointed at the approach of the referees. They seemed to be allowing all sorts of violence as legal against the ball carrier. When the game ended, Pelé's legs ached from top to bottom because he had been kicked and hit so much. The rumor going around the stadium was that the head of the FIFA, who was British, ordered the whistle-blowers to referee laxly and let the defenders take things where they may.

Against his will, Pelé was rested the next game and Brazil fell to Hungary 3–1. In the group standings, Brazil trailed both Hungary and Portugal and was in danger of not advancing to the medal round. Brazil was in a difficult position. It not only had to beat Portugal, but had to win by a large goal margin. The team delayed and delayed announcing the starting lineup and Pelé was angry that the players which the team fielded had not even all played together in practice because of the split training groups. "It would have been a ridiculous situation on the most inexperienced teams in an infantile league," Pelé steamed. "Here, in World Cup competition against one of the strongest teams of the tournament, it was suicidal."[3]

While fans back home may have been wringing their hands with worry, they did not really know what was going on. They expected the Brazilians to rise to the occasion with a huge victory. Inside the closed circle of the team, however, Pelé recognized the operation as being in disarray and broken beyond repair. It was too late to correct the mistakes that piled up over the months leading to the Cup. For Brazil, it was one-and-done elimination as the rest of the world played on, unless it could produce a magnificent result.

One of Portugal's assets was Eusebio, indisputably one of the best players in the world and someone whom his home fans touted as the very best, even better than Pelé. Pelé was over the hill, they said, and this was the keen young player spoiling to replace him as the king of soccer.

Eusebio de Silva Ferreira was born in Mozambique, but played his international career with Portugal. In the 1966 Cup, he was awarded the Bronze Ball Award, emblematic of being the best player in the tournament. He scored nine goals. The year before the Cup event, Eusebio won the Ballon d'Or, the award for the best soccer player of the year in Europe. He was actually only two years younger than Pelé, but was newer to the international scene. Interestingly, as someone who was a black player in a white country, but someone greatly admired as an all-star, Eusebio drew the same nicknames as Pelé. He was also called the "Black Panther" at times and also the "Black Pearl." Both of those forms of compliments did highlight Pelé's race and the same applied to Eusebio.

During this World Cup competition, there were suggestions that Eusebio may have eclipsed Pelé in performance and was worthy of being called the best player in the world, if not the best player ever. If so, Eusebio was definitely not going to be the one to make the claim. He had too much respect and admiration for Pelé to engage in such a debate. It was a given that Eusebio had a better World Cup than Pelé, but Eusebio said that anyone who was writing Pelé off as a continuing great was being foolish. "I feel that calling me the new Pelé was very unfair both for Pelé and me," Eusebio said. "To me, Pelé is the greatest soccer player of all time. I only hope that one day I can be the second best ever."[4]

The Brazil–Portugal showdown was a critical event for the Brazilian team, but 14 minutes into the game, Portugal took a 1–0 lead. Eusebio was instrumental in setting up the goal. Another 11 minutes passed and Portugal raised its lead to 2–0. While Brazil did cut the margin to 2–1, Portugal rebounded for another goal and a 3–1 triumph. A distraught Pelé was also injured before the end of the game on a foul that was ignored and he had to be helped from the field. No doubt compounded by his frustration on the scoreboard, Pelé was infuriated by how opponents were able to kick and hit him without being whistled for fouls. The entire 1966 World Cup left a sour taste in his mouth.

Portugal was placed third, losing to host England in the semifinals, and England provoked joyous celebrations in the home of soccer by winning the World Cup over West Germany. When Brazil was eliminated without even reaching the quarterfinals, Pelé was irate. He despised the manner in which the Brazilian team had been managed—in his mind, a series of costly blunders—and he was furious at the way the World Cup games had been officiated, again in his mind, draining the beauty from the sport. He never got over those feelings and announced that if that's the way things were going to work, he would not play in another World Cup tournament. "I was completely disgusted with what happened in 1966, and today, more than 10 years later, I still am," he said in 1977. "After that game I swore I would never play in another World Cup game. I would stay in Santos and play for the Santos club. I might or might not play with the Brazilian Selection in other than World Cup games, but the thankless job of playing for the Jules Rimet Trophy under the inept leadership of the Technical Commission . . . could be left to others."[5]

Since the Brazilian public had been led to believe from team leaders that the World Cup would be pretty much a stroll in an English park and their players would return home with the trophy and be ready for another parade, they were somewhat shocked by the ease with which Brazil was ejected from the tournament. Fans shook their heads in sorrow. Sportswriters wrote recriminations. Everyone was on the prowl to affix blame. How could everything go so wrong? In the end, the players on the field, not the administrators in the office, took the brunt of the criticism. While Pelé looked in another direction to place blame, he was very much in the maelstrom of intense scrutiny and analysis. As the best player, singled out in the past for considerable praise when the team did well, it was inevitable that Pelé would also be subjected to criticism when the team flopped.

There is no doubt that Pelé was expressing his frustration with the Brazil's team situation, organizers and game losses both, but that he was acting petulantly by declaring himself out of World Cup competition for good. He may have been right to complain about the loose style of refereeing that worked completely against him and his approach to the game, but he merely came off as a bad sport by making the blanket statement at the time he did. It was a rare time that Pelé was less than gracious in public on a matter regarding soccer, and really, about anything. The reaction reflected his depth of emotion about Brazil's defeat and also his own limited contributions.

Once again, it should be noted that in World Cup play, with a tournament only every four years, it takes a long time to make up for disappointment. In Pelé's case, he had two championships in the bank, and no one was going to be able to take those away, but with the passage of another four years before the next competition, he was going to move into athletic middle age. No one could predict the future. It was one thing to be able to say that Brazil would rebound in international play against various countries later that season or the next year. But no imagination could stretch four years ahead to see what type of team Brazil might have in 1970, who would be in charge of it in the front office, and who would be coaching it. Just like the Olympic Games, those who were crushed by disappointment, who performed at less than their expected best, had a long time to think about failing to finish first.

After Brazil's dismal performance at the World Cup in England, Pelé discovered when he returned home that, for the first time in his life, he had lost his enthusiasm for soccer. As a little boy, he showed pure joy playing in the streets without shoes and kicking a fake ball. All he wanted out of his life was to emulate his father, Dondinho. Each stop along the way, from neighborhood teams to local clubs, to joining Santos and then being selected for the national team, Pelé seemed to be following a scripted game plan of a wonderful life. Now, he had had a setback and it left him at loose ends. He was still only 26 years old but, actually for a short time, contemplated retirement.

One thing that lifted Pelé out of the doldrums was a scheduled club match between Santos and Eusebio's Portuguese club, Benfica. While it could not be attributed to this game alone, Pelé was working on remotivating himself. The old statement about not getting mad, but getting even was applied to some degree. Pelé was mad about Brazil's loss and he did want to get even, too. While this sort of game was a completely different type of contest than countries meeting in the World Cup, it represented a certain genius of scheduling. Both clubs' managements were aware that the public wanted to see Pelé and Eusebio on the same pitch again. Certainly, no one equated the value of team victory with a World Cup confrontation, but the idea that the two best players in the world would share the same field excited the imagination, made for good theater, good entertainment, and was something the public clamored for.

Most assuredly, Brazilian fans would want to see such a match in Sao Paulo and Portuguese fans would want to see such a match in Lisbon. The organizers might have sold 100,000 tickets if they had a venue large enough. But most peculiarly to the rabid soccer fans of Europe and South America, the game was slated to be played in New York at Downing Stadium on Randall's Island. The stadium theoretically held about 22,000 fans.

It was all about marketing. The teams were persuaded to bring big-time soccer to the United States to show it off and television could take care of showing the rest of the world. This was Pelé's first appearance in the ancient stadium that dated back to the 1930s, but unbeknown to him at the time and to soccer fans, it would become a very important place in his life. The stadium was jammed to overflowing on August 21, 1966, with paid attendance announced as 25,670—or standing room only. Alas, the fans, in an apparent attempt to match the worst of overseas fan behavior, were so rowdy that at least a dozen spectators needed medical attention. The worst of the activity, besides a small group of fans seeking to rush the field, involved the throwing of beer cans. At one point, the game was delayed for 15 minutes.

On the field, what promised to be an epic encounter between two of the world's best teams and the two best players in the world, turned out to be lopsided. Pelé and Santos completely dominated, winning 4–0. Pelé scored one goal and added three assists, setting up all the others. At one critical juncture—insult to injury—Pelé stole the ball off Eusebio's foot. His performance, and the result, was taken as proof that Pelé was nowhere near washed up and that Eusebio, while great, was no Pelé.

Eusebio, of course, had always been circumspect in giving Pelé his appropriate notices and had not been the one to anoint himself as king, only read about it like others in newspapers. "I told you not to discredit Pelé," Eusebio told sportswriters after the game. "He's still as great as ever and he'll stay that way until he decides to retire."[6]

The head-to-head nature of the Pelé–Eusebio game was more like what American football fans think of when two star quarterbacks lead their teams into a playoff game. Yet another game on the trip to the United States provided a larger forum for Pelé to be showcased. It was no secret that the United States was ridiculously behind much smaller and less well-off nations in soccer than stood to reason. The main case was the focus and support for other sports that were more popular and attracted the best American athletes. Soccer was viewed as a niche sport, primarily followed by immigrants who moved to the United States from nations where the game was popular and they transferred their allegiance to their new home in the same manner they toted suitcases with their clothing.

Indeed, when soccer began making inroads and began showing staying power with the leagues that kept being formed and then folding, it was built on the backs of those very supporters who had come from far away and missed the sport. On this tour, however, which pitted Pelé and Eusebio, Santos also met Internationale of Italy in Yankee Stadium. While there may not have been a huge number of Brazilians residing in New York in 1966, there were plenty of Italians. The game attracted 42,000 fans, which stood as an American soccer attendance record for a number of years. It was about this time, in October 1966, that *Sports Illustrated*, pretty much the only U.S. mainstream media that cared about sports such as soccer, splashed a very lengthy article about Pelé across the pages of the magazine. This was significant in a number of ways. *Sports Illustrated* was one of a very small number of sports publications with any type of national influence. *Sports Illustrated* prided itself on being ahead of trends in even the most minor of sports, and the headline was designed to wake up complacent American sports fans and tell them what they were missing. It read: "The Most Famous Athlete In The World."

Some sports fans huffed, "I doubt that." They simply did not know better, did not grasp soccer's hold on so many countries. They had never lived in nations where those residents would have said, "Who's that?" about Bob Cousy, the Boston Celtics basketball star, or Mickey Mantle, the New York Yankees' baseball star. They just didn't understand that soccer was the world's sport.

The story, thousands of words long, was the first major attempt to paint a picture of Pelé for U.S. sports fans and it was very flattering. Pelé was portrayed as being very modest while talking about his accomplishments, almost always smiling on the field, an individual who could single-handedly take control of a game and reshape the pace of play and create openings that were previously closed as if walled off by a jail cell's bars. All of it was true and accurate and well-known to Brazilian, South American, and European soccer fans—people for whom soccer was on the same importance level with inhaling. To some degree, Pelé came across as someone as perfect as a Boy Scout piling up merit badges.

The author, Pete Axthelm, a well-known writer of the day, seemed taken with Pelé, reporting that the player was "cautious and soft-spoken, less concerned with his records than with showing you what a nice guy a superstar can be."[7]

It was not in his nature anyway, but Pelé had long ago learned how to deal with sportswriters, and so he was not about to issue any controversial statements to the American reporter. Nor did he break character and begin to gloat and brag about how great he was. "Luck," said Pelé. "You need a lot of luck to have a long and successful career. There is so much chance of injury, or of something suddenly going wrong. But so far I've been as lucky as anyone. I'm very fortunate."[8]

At that time, Pelé was making about $200,000 in soccer salary and swelling his earnings to about $500,000 a year through endorsements. He was a very good provider for his family and while there must have been some jealousy out there among other soccer players, they could not gripe because Pelé pretty much deserved all he could get. He simply towered over the game.

For decades, the image of soccer in the provinces, whether in poorer Latin American countries, or rough-edged European countries, was one tinged with danger. The sport was not actively covered by major metropolitan newspapers in the United States, but periodically, a blurb would appear that used the term "soccer riot." Fans apparently killed their athletes with kindness in some places. It was reported how English soccer fields, and some elsewhere, were surrounded by moats to prevent the crazed masses from climbing over fences or stoned walls to get to their "heroes" and tear them limb from limb with hard-hitting hugs.

While Pelé appeared every inch the gentleman, he had experienced these scenarios as well. Some fans overseas merely wanted a glimpse of Pelé beyond the pitch. It would have been risking his life to offer it in Senegal, where the bus taking him to the airport at 4:00 A.M. was surrounded by well-wishers, or in Italy, where a crowd waited for hours for him to appear and he waited it out in hiding. Another time, in Caracas, Santos waited four hours for a mob to be cleared so the team could board its airplane. There were few places in the world where Pelé could walk down the street unrecognized and unmolested. The United States was actually one of them because of that public soccer blindness.

Once, on the road from the airport to Abidjan in the Ivory Coast of Africa, about 15,000 soccer fans lined Pelé's path. He rode past them in a convertible-roofed car with his hands in the air. "It was like a parade for a president," said Julio Mazzei, one of Pelé's best friends and, at the time, Santos' team trainer.[9]

If Pelé grew tense or nervous when confronted with such mobs that merely wanted a glimpse of him, he rarely let on. If he thought it ridiculous that thousands of people would interrupt their day and wander into a street to honor him, he never let on about that. "Yes, I would like more privacy," Pelé said, "a chance to move around and go places without causing a disturbance. But the attention is a compliment. When the crowds stop coming, then it will be time to worry."[10]

For the moment, for the time being, at least, Pelé was like the Beatles, pursued by screaming fans wherever he appeared.

NOTES

1. Pelé, My Life in Pictures (New York: Simon & Schuster, 2008), p. 47.

2. Ibid.

3. Pelé and Robert L. Fish, My Life and the Beautiful Game (New York: Doubleday & Company, 1977), p. 195.

4. Bill Gutman, Pelé (New York: Grosset & Dunlap, 1976), p. 12.

5. Pelé and Fish, p. 197.

6. Don Kowet, Pelé (New York: Atheneum, 1976), p. 56.

7. Pete Axthelm, "The Most Famous Athlete in the World," Sports Illustrated, October 24, 1966.

8. Ibid.

9. Ibid.

10. Ibid.

Chapter 7

MORE THAN A
SOCCER PLAYER

As an adult, as opposed to being a daydreaming youth, Pelé discovered that there was more to life than kicking a ball. Never as a kid did he imagine that he would one day be acclaimed as the best soccer player in the world or the best soccer player who ever lived. And, even if he had, he would not have begun to contemplate the responsibilities that were attendant to being the claimant to such a lofty title, or the responsibilities that simply came with being a man.

Once his faith in a friend to handle his money proved to be misplaced, Pelé had to become more of a businessman. Although he pretty much preferred just to be a full-time soccer player and he certainly had not trained himself to be a financial expert, Pelé knew he could not hold himself aloof from this kind of personal business.

In addition, Pelé was a husband to Rosemeri, and the father of two children. He had to make sure they were provided for, but also that they were protected from his celebrityhood and led the most normal of lives possible. Still, he had to worry about them being safe from any types of threats that might appear unexpectedly simply because he was their famous father.

As someone who was loyal, believed in a sense of propriety, acting with class and staying clear of anything that might besmirch his reputation, Pelé also imposed a high standard of behavior on himself. It would not do to be caught in embarrassing situations or any situation at all that would diminish the import of the name Pelé. He had been blessed by God with these skills in a sport that millions loved and he owed it to everyone to make the best and proper use of them.

While Pelé felt strongly about fair play and the implicit fairness of the game, he did not wish to impose his personal beliefs on the public at large, whether it came to religion or politics. To him, those were very much personal matters, not topics to campaign about. One thing that Pelé learned, however, was that he was such a singular figure in soccer that as he traveled the world to country after country, the leaders of those countries, regardless of their own political leanings, wanted to meet with him, shake his hand, or dine with him.

Presidents, prime ministers, kings, princes, shahs, and dictators, too, wanted to make sure they met the world's greatest soccer player if he crossed their borders. He did not choose to make political stands, rejecting the approaches of any leader for political cause. Pelé did not think that was his place when visiting their country. After all, he had come to them, so it behooved him to be polite. Politeness is how he saw his role, his presence on their soil not endorsing their policies. He may have been a citizen of the world as much as Brazil, but he was not a political or government leader who was going to change the world in any way except by providing a bit of entertainment. More than once, Pelé said simply that if he made others happy, then he was happy.

During one of his earliest visits to the United States, Pelé met President Richard Nixon. Some years later, he would kick a soccer ball around with President Gerald Ford. In 1962, the Duke of Edinburgh, Prince Philip, was on an official diplomatic trip to Brazil, and while in the country, very much wanted to see Pelé play in a game. Of course, he also wanted to meet Pelé face-to-face. While the arrangers of such a mission fretted over what the proper protocol would be when the two men encountered one another, the prince took care of it by descending to the field to consummate a hand shake. "If a prime minister or a king wishes to meet me, I gladly go to a palace for lunch or some talk," Pelé said. "But I do not mix with politics or religion. I am Brazilian, but I feel everywhere at home."[1]

There are athletes and there are stars, and Pelé was both. He had charisma and star power and he came to learn that early on. Some of it was due to his easygoing personality, the image fans had of him smiling on the field all of the time, and some of it was his spectacular body control and instinct for the game that led him to create goals as if he was an artist, a painter creating a vision. In 1961, Pelé was playing a game for Santos against the Fluminese club of Rio at the Maracana, the immense stadium in Rio de Janeiro that holds almost 200,000 fans. The showplace soccer stadium of the country is currently being rebuilt in advance of the 2014 World Cup, but for young boys growing up in the 1950s and 1960s, it was the place to play, the most famous arena in the country.

During that game on March 5, 1961, Pelé scored a goal that was so fantastic that it was permanently commemorated. Pelé gained control of the ball in his own team's penalty area and one-by-one as Rio defenders charged at him, he slipped the ball around them with footwork. He advanced through the entire opposing team and booted home a shot. A local newspaper called it "the most beautiful goal ever scored in the Maracana" and footed the bill to install a plaque marking the occasion. "It was a great honor," Pelé said, "and one of which I am very proud."[2]

Pelé was always doing something larger than life, usually revolving around scoring the impossible goal. Showing up after being advertised was also an important role for Pelé. People planned their lives around a Pelé appearance. Occasionally, they even planned their deaths around a Pelé appearance.

In 1967, Santos toured Africa, making stops in the Congo, Gabon, Benin, the Ivory Coast, and Nigeria. There was only one problem in Nigeria. The country was in the middle of a civil war. The self-proclaimed Republic of Biafra was seeking to secede from Nigeria and this was definitely a shooting war. There was danger everywhere and starvation and other hardships throughout the land. Powerful emotions were at issue and powerful beliefs were at the core. Yet, for a visit from the great Pelé in order to play an exhibition soccer game, a ceasefire was declared so people on both sides of the conflict could witness his skills. After playing for the Nigerian citizens and army, Pelé received an escort to the midpoint of a bridge over a river that was the dividing line between the national boundary and the revolutionaries' boundary. A Nigerian captain turned Pelé over to his counterpart among the enemy. Once Pelé's visit ended, the two sides went back to shooting at one another.

The stop in Nigeria/Biafra was Pelé's first visit to Africa. The black Africans embraced Pelé like a deity, and for once, he thought about the color of his skin. He had traveled thousands of miles around the world, but only once before touched down on the continent—a brief visit to Egypt. There was something different, a bit more special about this tour for him.

"It was with very strong and strange emotions that I first saw Africa," Pelé said. "Everywhere I went I was looked upon and treated as a god, almost certainly because I represented to blacks in those countries what a black man could accomplish in a country where there was little racial prejudice, as well as providing physical evidence that a black man could become rich, even in a white man's country. To these people, who had little possibility of ever escaping the crushing poverty in which they found themselves, I somehow represented a ray of hope, however faint."[3]

As Santos and Pelé moved about from country to country, the scene duplicated itself, a surreal level of enthusiasm, of hero worship, engulfing them as thousands of people in each destination surrounded their plane, crammed stadiums, and cheered their presence even more strongly than they cheered their play. At each stadium, the circumstances repeated themselves, with the police or army in uniform holding back mobs, guiding the leader of the country to Pelé so he could have a few words. Only one thing went wrong. In Dakar, Senegal, Pelé scored two goals on a particular goal-tender, who then burst into tears and inconsolably fled the field. It bothered Pelé that the man was so crushed, felt so humiliated in his home, that he tried to visit him in his locker room to say a few encouraging words. But the man would not meet with him and Pelé said he was haunted by the situation for a long time. He had not intended to shame the man, only do what he had done so many times before in so many locations— score goals.

Pelé had a strong effect on people, but above all, he seemed to relate well to children. He always thought of himself as a sort of ragamuffin of a kid and projected that image onto other children when he came across them in groups or singly. There was something in his makeup that children sensed, a feeling of sensitivity toward them. There are some famous people who exude warmth to people of all ages and Pelé was one of them. Adults may react to such an athlete's fame, but children up to a certain age seem to react more instinctively to someone. Some might be so young or sheltered that they had to be told Pelé was a well-known soccer player, but for those children, an adult taking an interest in them was a big deal.

Whenever the circumstances offered opportunity, Pelé stopped what he was doing to sign autographs for children. He did not sigh and indicate it was a hardship to do so, but it was something he eagerly waded into. One day, a fence was between Pelé and a crowd of youngsters and his friend Dr. Julio Mazzei, the Santos trainer, watched as Pelé, who had a barrier between himself and the kids, making it easy to avoid them, instead chose to join them. He was leaving the stadium and a barricade held back hundreds of kids. "That," he said, "is the future of soccer in this country, not us." That's when Mazzei marveled at Pelé taking the initiative to meet the kids. "The children," Mazzei said, "the little ones who have never seen him play, are drawn to him. They come calling 'Pe-lay, Pe-lay,' to touch him, to be near him. They have no fear of him. A long time ago I realized that it will never be possible to say what makes Pelé Pelé."[4]

Sometimes, Pelé was such a drawing card at an away game that his mere presence excited the locals into demonstrations. This was particularly emphasized once when an official threw him out of a game. This was a bit like going to the theater and discovering that an understudy was playing Hamlet that day instead of Nicol Williamson, who had the sniffles. If the attendees threatened to burn down the building, Williamson might crawl out of bed to take the stage after all. This was not a perfect parallel, but during a 1969 game in Bogota, Colombia, members of the host club attempted to rile Pelé and two other black Santos strikers with racial insults.

A furious Pelé took his case to the head official, but instead of incurring a crackdown on the opponents' behavior, he was thrown out of the game. While he was starting to remove his shoes in the locker room, however, Pelé was chased down and ordered to return to the field. When the fans realized what his disappearance meant, they were so inflamed they indulged in the beginnings of a riot. They were setting fire to their seat cushions and hurling them onto the field. Police intervention overruled the official, Pelé was summoned to the game, and the official was thrown out.

As the seasons passed, Santos' team management kept up its aggressive scheduling and marketing, always prepared to travel thousands of miles to appear in games against clubs that appreciated Pelé as a drawing card. There is no question the team played for the money in easy-to-reach and out-of-the-way places. A tour may take Santos to a large American city or to a remote desert outpost. Santos couldn't quite match the all-time traveling sports kings, the Harlem Globetrotters, but the Brazilian club most assuredly did its share of globetrotting. Depending on the opponent, sometimes Pelé was treated like the kind of movie star whose name appears on the marquee above the title of the picture. So instead of advertising Santos versus another team, the advertising featured Pelé's name in the largest letters, or at least in emphasis.

On August 4, 1968, Santos was scheduled to meet an American soccer club at the Oakland Alameda County Coliseum. The local affiliate advertised the match this way in an ad that was roughly 8x10 inches in size. It read, "International Soccer . . . Oakland Clippers vs. Santos of Brazil." Underneath that heading, there was a large, square photograph featuring Pelé making a header pass. A square-inch box superimposed on the photo read, "Pelé . . . King of Soccer." Underneath that in bold letters was the phrase, "SEE THE WORLD's GREATEST SOCCER STAR." Prices for adults in advance sale were just $4. It was difficult to miss the focus: the great and wonderful Pelé was coming and there will also be a soccer game between your local club and this foreign team.

Santos knew how its bread was buttered, of course. Without Pelé in the lineup, the club would not have been in demand around the world. Most importantly, since it is imperative that a team defend its own turf first, in the first 20 years of its existence, Santos had won two league titles. But in the first nine years of Pelé's association with Santos, the club had won seven titles. That's taking care of business at home, too.

One of the finest and most satisfying seasons for Pelé and Santos was 1968. Wherever Santos traveled, it won matches, tournaments, cups, trophies, anything that was at stake. Pelé called this "a new golden period. We won all five major competitions we entered, picking up titles in Chile, Argentina, the South American Inter-Club in Brazil, and more. We played in six countries, with a win-to-game ratio that was second to none. The foot-balling machine was better than ever. Journalists from Brazil and abroad acknowledged that Santos was the greatest team in the world. We'd walk out on the pitch and acknowledge the crowd by bowing to them respectfully. Everything we did was copied and this was good for the spectacle of football."[5]

That was part of Pelé's appeal. What he did, his style of play, was good for the spectacle of football. He was a magician with his feet, able to balance, control and kick a ball in ways that could move entire stadiums to sounds they never thought they could make. He inspired young soccer players who wanted to be like him. He was graceful and talented, what he accomplished was easily visible, if not easily emulated, and it benefited the sport because what he specialized in made people swoon. He was not known for clutching and grabbing, kicking opponents, or hitting them hard. He was the target much more often, which also put the crowd on his side. Spectators resented it if teams contained and defended Pelé, especially if they used desperate means. Pelé was a thrill machine and the fans wanted thrills and chills.

It was part of the sportswriters' duty to not only describe what they saw, but explain what it meant, so they were forever searching for the meaning of Pelé, the root cause of what separated him from all others. One French writer pursued the theme that Pelé was a genius on the pitch. He consulted Webster's dictionary and reported the definition of genius as "Extraordinary power of invention or origination of any kind." For those who only thought it applied to schoolwork, such as mathematics or language study in the sense that children call their contemporaries a genius because they receive all "A's," the French author took the matter farther. "We often characterize genius in opposition to talent," he said. "Genius is inborn, intuitive, instinctive, creative. Talent stems from reasoned intelligence and constant effort at improvement. Talent repeats flawlessly what has already been done, it does not create." Examined was a 65-yard shot made by Pelé that at first the fans considered to be a crazy attempt. When it went in, they were amazed and gave credit to Pelé for even thinking of taking it.[6]

Perhaps that was a definition of genius in sport—an athlete that confronts the impossible and sees the possible.

In the late 1960s, when Santos made a second tour of the United States, Pelé formed some stronger opinions about the country. To most of the world, the United States was still a vast wasteland for soccer. The caliber of play did not come close to matching that of Europe or South America, and for the most part, most Americans didn't care anyway. However, due to his longevity at the top of the sport, more than a decade at this point, Pelé found that his name was known in certain circles. The reception was nothing like that of what he had experienced in Africa. There were no delirious American mobs just wishing to touch the hem of his garment or screaming girls that were enamored of the British rock and roll bands that had taken over the radio airwaves and salivated to meet the guitarists and drummers who produced those 45-rpm records. The intensity of interest fell far short of that, yet still, the feeling and mood was different, the awareness keener, the appreciation for top-notch soccer greater.

"It was true that I could walk down the street without having anyone recognize me," Pelé said, "which was a pleasure, and I could eat in a restaurant without having a crowd besiege me for autographs, and without the waiter pointing me out to the other patrons as if I were a special attraction brought in by the management. Still, the name Pelé was known to far more people than I would have imagined. I came to realize that America was a vast reservoir for future association football."[7]

Pelé was pleased that his name was known and Santos' name was known wherever they traveled. He knew his World Cup history and knew that the United States had participated in the first World Cup competition in 1930 and even won a couple of games before apparently losing interest in the sport. He sensed that with its devotion to sport, its wealth and stature in the world, the United States could be the sleeping giant of soccer. But only if someone worked really hard to build upon the weak foundation. For Pelé, during that visit, it was merely a sociological observation. He did not envision any role for himself in this mythical U.S. expansion into the world of soccer. "I could see despite this seeming lack of interest in the sport in the United States, all the game needed was an impetus to bring the United States back into the fold, to make the game as popular here as it was in the rest of the world," Pelé said. [8]

But the world's greatest soccer player did not for a moment believe he would have anything whatsoever to do with making that happen. He was a Brazilian living far, far away and he was not going to move out of Brazil.

As Pelé's career marched on, he became an almost superhuman figure. He helped his nation win two World Cup championships. He led the nation in scoring almost every year. He collected unprecedented rewards. It was all dazzling. For most, it is a special distinction to become widely known in their home community. For the rare individual, he reaches unsurpassed heights as a national figure. To become known throughout the world, to be informed your face is the best-known among the billions of people who live on the planet, to be told that you are the best at something in the entire world and then later to be anointed as the best that ever lived at what you do, is a mind-boggling experience. The reaction to such god-like status can go one of two ways—the individual may become insufferably arrogant or be humbled so thoroughly that he is constantly on alert to remind himself that he is just like everyone else.

Pelé lives the life of a world-class figure, yet inside, he remains to some degree the poor boy who overcame the poverty of his upbringing. It always seemed a bit unreal to him when manufacturers sought to plaster his face or his words on their products, endorsing them. Eventually, there was Pelé saying positive things about brands of clothing, shoes, watches, bicycles, soccer equipment, and even chocolate bars. Back in Three Hearts, where he lived a portion of his early life, a street was named after him. So was an 80,000-seat soccer stadium.

Both spiritual riches and literal riches came his way. As much as it was possible to do so, Pelé stayed on the good side of everyone, the average soccer fan, the national politicians, the officials governing his sport, and the press. It was not always easy and he was sometimes criticized. No one is perfect and sometimes, no doubt, situations arose where he deserved to be chastened. Pelé always tried to do right and live up to his principles, and occasionally, such as when it was reported that he was holding out for a $20,000 appearance fee to a big event, he was treated unfairly. Furious over the slight, Pelé said that he had not been guilty of such a faux pas, and he never would have considered even asking for such a payment.

If anyone believed that Pelé could do more to uplift poor people in the country, he sometimes replied that he was not a politician and did not figure in any such policy decisions. Yet, when an issue revolved around helping children, he made himself available. Sometimes during interviews, he would spontaneously blurt that people should "not forget the fate of poor children."[9]

Pelé was a man who could cry in public and, sometimes, the cause of the tears was regret stemming from a sad situation arising from awareness of children being deprived. Poor children, ill children, children who suffered, they all could draw tears. Sometimes, Pelé gave money to help children and, sometimes, his presence visiting a hospital improved their morale. At games, when children flocked around him seeking autographs, he tried to accommodate everyone.

Throughout his illustrious soccer career, Pelé was always generous with his time when it came to paying attention to children who admired him. Sometimes that meant signing autographs and other times that meant visiting sick children in hospitals. (AP Photo/Harris)

Late in his career, when he was playing in the United States, he incurred an injury and could not play in a home game. He arrived at Downing Stadium separately from his teammates in a limousine because he was sidelined. When he swung the door open near the players' entrance, he was instantly swarmed by about 30 youngsters. Pelé said he would sign for them, but apologized for not being able to play for them because of his torn hamstring. He told them to return a week later to see him in action.

"I appreciate the crowds around me," Pelé said, "especially the kids. I know that when I was growing up soccer was one of the few things I could enjoy. Seeing a top player was always a thrill. Now I get the thrill myself by having the kids around me."[10]

For those who spent time around Pelé, who saw him in action on the field, and watched him mingle with his fans, there was always a hint dropped that the man still retained many elements of a little boy. He wanted to make friends with the other kids. He attacked his role in the game with the enthusiasm of a player just starting out, not the veteran that he was. This all contributed to the charm of Pelé. He never wanted anyone to go away disappointed, either because he let down in a game, or they were offended by something he did off the field.

Above all, one thing Pelé made very clear in his newspaper interviews, in his talks to people, when he spoke his mind, was that he never forgot where he came from, never was he going to bury his past and pretend he was someone born into the aristocracy. Pelé would always remember the poverty and the hard times and the hard work that lifted him above it all and carved out this fascinating life.

NOTES

1. Don Kowet, *Pelé* (New York: Atheneum, 1976), p. 82.

2. Harry Harris, *Pelé: His Life and Times* (New York: Welcome Rain Publishers, 2001), p. 61.

3. Pelé and Robert L. Fish, *My Life and the Beautiful Game* (New York: Doubleday & Company, 1977), p. 203.

4. Kowet, p. 86.

5. Pelé, *My Life in Pictures* (New York: Simon & Schuster, 2008), p. 51.

6. François Thebaud, *Pelé* (New York: Harper & Row Publishers, 1976), pp. 77–78.

7. Pelé and Fish, p. 205.

8. Ibid., p. 206.

9. Thebaud, p. 112.

10. Kowet, p. 123.

Chapter 8

1,000 GOALS

Soccer fans grew used to seeing Pelé do things that had never been done before. Most of the time, that meant watching him torque his body into a shape that created an unusual angle to shoot a ball at a goaltender. Other times, that meant admiring the supersonic speed with which a kick flew at a net-minder's head. And, sometimes, it plain just meant dropping open their jaws in disbelief as Pelé dribbled past four or five defenders, inevitably leading to a goal.

Those all represented individual moments, a snapshot of a play, a stunning maneuver that no one else had ever before managed or imagined. But during the 1969 season, sportswriters who had mastered the use of a calculator, or abacus, pointed out to soccer fans that Pelé was about to achieve something fresh and different that had also never been accomplished by another soccer player. The pride of Brazil was closing in on the 1,000th goal of his storied career.

As long as he stayed healthy (always an issue for an athlete) and scored at his usual blistering pace, it was figured that Pelé could reach this previously unachieved total sometime in the mid-to-late autumn of the year. By October, Pelé's career number had climbed to 989 goals. He was indeed closing in on a remarkable milestone.

"It became *the* story of the year," Pelé noted. Because he was Pelé and because he was known throughout the world, the entire soccer world paid attention. A few years later, in a quest that mesmerized American sports fans, the Atlanta Braves' Hank Aaron would crush his 715th career home run to surpass the indomitable Babe Ruth to claim Major League baseball's most cherished record. In the context of American life, what Aaron accomplished was huge. But because baseball at that time was pretty much only a national pastime, not a worldwide one, the focus on Aaron was mostly limited to the United States. [1]

Not so with Pelé. Soccer was very much a worldwide game and Pelé had proven over and over again that he had a worldwide following. His singular achievement captured the attention of soccer fans everywhere and they tried their best to keep track goal by goal as his total rose. "The press, locally and nationally, seemed to talk about nothing else," Pelé said. Yes, he was in the vortex of a hurricane, but how could he expect anything different? This was a tremendous soccer achievement. He was striving for a milestone that no other player had come close to and that fans would recall forever. So, it was going to be accompanied with more than the usual fanfare of just about any kind of soccer development short of World Cup victories. "At each Santos game there were hordes of reporters." [2]

After hitting that 989 total, Pelé splurged, went on a goal-spending spree, so to speak, scoring four in one game against the club Portuguesa. While crossing above 990 put him in a frame of mind to reach 1,000, the pressure also ratcheted up. It was almost a tangible atmospheric change. A week after that, Pelé scored two goals in a match against Coritiba. He crept ever closer to the magic number. He notched another goal against Flamenco an additional week later.

Each time Pelé played the carloads of reporters followed him to a new destination. It was not clear how long it would take for him to score the precious goal. He could explode and go over the top with a four-goal game, or he could chip away at the remaining numbers, collecting a single goal at a time and, in essence, string out the pursuit of the milestone for more weeks. He would have been happy to solve everyone's problem and get it over with and send everyone back home if it was within his power. One goal at a time was how things were working out, however, and the traveling crew of reporters had pages in their newspapers to fill, so they wrote story after story about the impending special moment.

The greatest anticlimax of all would be if Pelé reached number 999 and stopped scoring, whether because he suddenly lost his touch or he got injured. That would again be making a parallel with Aaron, who did experience just about the worst kind of delay in his chase of Ruth. Aaron's 1973 season ended with him one home run short of tying Ruth. He had to wait through an entire winter, an entire off-season, to tie and then surpass him. Pelé was not chasing anyone, but his destination was just as numerically certain.

In a November 1969 game against Recife, Pelé scored two goals. Two more goals were needed to reach the mountaintop. Sportswriters had been on his trail for weeks, but now that he was so close they could taste it and actually increased the hyperbole of stories. Pelé became wide-eyed reading about himself. "It was said that scoring 1,000 goals would make me immortal," Pelé said. "Nonsense, of course, but I did feel the pressure."[3]

Anyone made of flesh and blood would feel the pressure. The eyes of the world were on Pelé, the eyes of his friends and family, his team-mates, his countrymen, fans of Santos. That was also true when millions tuned into World Cup action, but this was different. This was not about winning for Brazil, it was about scoring a goal for his own resume. It felt odd to Pelé that there was such a hubbub over a number. He was underestimating what the 1,000th goal meant to people. He knew that he was just a man and not someone who was immortal, otherwise he wouldn't pull muscles, sprain ankles, or strain knee ligaments. Still, he did understand how the nice round number would be something people would remember. Of course, he had no intentions of stopping there. Pelé did not plan to walk off the pitch after scoring the 1,000th goal and retire. He was going to play on and as long as he was healthy enough to play, he assumed he would score more goals.

Even Pelé started to call this road show a traveling circus by this time as games were catalogued, miles mounted, and he inched closer to the coveted goal. Standing just two goals shy of the mark, Santos and Pelé arrived in Joao Pessoa for a match against the local club Botafogo. A stunning scene greeted them. Even before the game was to be played, Pelé was received like a conquering general home from the wars, with

Santos players his honor guard. The airport was overrun with thousands of people seeking a glimpse of Pelé.

"They were cheering as if the celebration party had begun," Pelé said, "as if I had already achieved the result. The local politicians made a real song and dance about me. I was given the title of 'Citizen of Joao Pessoa.' They were obviously keen that I score the 1,000th goal right there."[4]

Pelé was more than ready to oblige. This had become a wearying quest. As great a player as Pelé was, he could not turn his talent off and on like a water faucet and wish a goal into the net now any more than he had been able to pull off such a feat in the preceding years.

During the contest itself, Santos had little trouble controlling the opposition. The score was 2–0 when Santos was awarded a penalty kick. Under ordinary circumstances, Carlos Alberto, another all-time great Brazilian player, handled the penalty kick duties for the team. Alberto insisted that Pelé take a turn. Although this was exactly the type of situation where Pelé did not want any special treatment, Alberto made a persuasive argument. Surrounded as they were by a vociferous crowd roaring for Pelé to take the shot, Alberto and the other Santos players told Pelé that if he did not take the shot, the team would be blamed and the fans might not let them escape from the stadium in one piece.

"I was not the team's regular penalty taker," Pelé said. "I have taken a few penalties in my career, but neither in the national team, nor at Santos, was I the first choice. I always say that if I had been I would have got to 1,000 goals much quicker. So I caved in and put the ball on the spot. Whack. My 999th goal. One to go."[5]

Plenty of time remained in the game, so it seemed possible that Pelé might yet wrap up the pursuit of the 1,000th goal on the spot. However, in a fluke occurrence, Santos' goalie took ill and had to come out of the game. It was a little known fact to the public since it came up so rarely, but Pelé was the team's back-up goalie, so he had to move to the net, eliminating his scoring chances. In all, Pelé said he filled in as a reserve goalie four times over the years for Santos and even once for the national team, although it was in a friendly, not a critical tournament or championship.

Up until this point in soccer history, no player had ever come close to collecting 1,000 goals, so it was an international novelty and the eyes of the soccer world were definitely upon Pelé during the final weeks of the chase. He recognized that this was a great story for the soccer world, but "personally it made me very nervous. I would have been pleased to have been informed one morning that the day before I had scored the 1,000th goal, but to have it ahead of me, and referred to daily in newspapers or on the radio was unnerving." Pelé said he felt as if he was "a slide under a microscope" and he was pretty sure the attention was getting to his teammates, too.[6]

After Pelé pulled within one goal of the 1,000 plateau, the attention was even more magnified, something which surprised him since he didn't think that was possible. A mid-November game against the Esporte club offered his first chance to set the record with a single goal.

"I think we probably had every radio in the country tuned into the game," Pelé said. "When I came out onto the field I felt nervous. I had long wished the 1,000th goal was over and done with, but never as much as on this day. I had a sudden cold feeling that I was doomed to go for years and years without scoring another goal. That elusive Goal Number 1,000 would always be in front of me, taunting me, and preventing me from playing proper football."[7]

While that was a nightmare, not reality, Pelé did not obtain his 1,000th goal that day. Even more frustrating, near the end of the game, he smashed a shot that the goalie could not reach, but which did not go in. It struck the crossbar and bounced away.

The drama only increased as Santos moved around the country fulfilling its schedule. Next up was Vasco da Gama in Rio de Janeiro and that meant the confrontation would take place in Maracana Stadium. That certainly was an appropriate location for such a milestone if Pelé could score. Soccer fans believed the same because they turned out 80,000 strong and sat through pouring rain that might otherwise have deterred them from attending.

Increasing the challenge was the fact that the Rio team featured a defensive player of superb stature named Rene, whose sole job that day was to shadow Pelé and try to interfere with any Santos passes headed in his direction. Rene played brilliantly and held Pelé at bay. He rarely was able to touch the ball, never mind get off a shot. If the fans were displeased, Rene was merely doing his job, as if his team was announcing, "Not against us."

By this point, Pelé was starting to think almost superstitiously, that his scoring the 1,000th goal was not meant to be. "I was beginning to think that the number 1,000 was a jinx," he said, "and that maybe God never intended that anyone should ever score 1,000 goals."[8]

Before the game, players on the other team teased Pelé, though it was not apparent if they were being serious or not, and they kept telling him that he would not score against them that day. The reality was that Vasco da Gama was going to play hard, play to win, and do everything it could to stop Pelé from scoring. They would applaud him from afar if he scored his 1,000th goal against another team, but the players just didn't want him to get it against them.

Rain, mugginess, it did not matter. The huge crowd that came to see Santos play Vasco da Gama was really there with one purpose on its mind. There was no great concern about who won or lost that night. There was nothing that mattered except that at some point during the 90 minutes of action, Pelé put the ball into the net via head or foot, no one cared, but somehow, a legal shot attributed to him had to go up on the scoreboard. The fans had turned the scene into a special occasion. It was a mini-carnival, a very big day for scalpers asking skyrocketing prices for tickets, and for vendors selling souvenir buttons, banners, and king-sized photographs of the king. When Pelé ran out onto the field for team warm-ups, the hosts set off fireworks.

Rene's terrific defense stymied Pelé in the early going, but one reason Pelé was Pelé was because he was always able to exploit the slightest of advantages, the tiniest of openings. Even he said it was for only a split second when he freed himself from Rene and was able to control a pass. But it was not over. The goalie rose to the occasion and barely tipped the ball away with his fingertips.[9]

Pelé thought he had the goal and was down because he missed, but at the same time, the play helped shed his nerves. He felt much more like his old self, relieved of the tension, just out there on the field playing his game. What happened next was the type of odd play that leaves observers shaking their heads. Pelé was able to elude Rene once again after taking a pass, dashed in on net and boomed a kick. While it traveled a bit high and thumped off of the crossbar, Pelé was in position for a rebound to knock the ball in with his head. Rene had recovered and caught up to Pelé and also leapt and in his attempt to head the ball clear of the net, he accidentally knocked it in for a Santos score. It seemed impossible, but that fluke play interfered with what was Pelé's best chance to collect a goal for a few games.

Another opportunity presented itself. Pelé received a pass and saw just two defenders back, Rene and Fernando. He ran for the goal, guiding the ball with his feet and as he tried to split the defense, Fernando dove at him, making an illegal hit. The referee called for a penalty kick. Some 13 minutes remained in the game. Of course, Pelé would take the kick, even though it was not in Santos' game plan. Once again, captain Carlos Alberto brooked no nonsense on this topic. Pelé had to fill the role. This faced him off against goalie Andrade and the suspense built as Pelé lingered, seeking an inner calmness that would help him take the perfect shot.

"A penalty kick certainly wasn't the way I had hoped to make my 1,000th goal, but at this point I would have taken it any I could just to get the affair over with," Pelé said. "I was trying to clear the cobwebs from my mind, trying to forget the importance of this one goal to me, to my game, to my team. Then, almost as if my body had gotten tired of waiting while my mind was still discussing the matter, I found I had kicked the ball and was watching it curve nicely past Andrade's outstretched fingers into the net." [10]

Goooooaaaaalllll! That was one of Pelé's favorite sayings as he pumped his fist in the air to mark his goals. Sometimes, he shouted it, and other times, he just thought it, but he enjoyed the sound of the exaggerated version of goal.

In baseball lore, the 1951 home run struck by the San Francisco Giants' Bobby Thomson to win the National League pennant over their rival Brooklyn Dodgers has forever been known as "the shot heard 'round the world." However, this truly was the shot heard around the world. The whole world was paying attention, waiting on Pelé's foot to make a statement. At last it did—1,000 goals! The milestone was reached on November 19, 1969. That happened to be a holiday, Brazil's national flag day. There was considerable flag waving on Pelé's behalf that day.

A pathfinder for most of his career, Pelé became the first soccer player to score 1,000 goals in his career and kept zooming past that total to end up with more than 1,200 goals when he retired. (AP Photo)

There had been a hush in the stadium as Pelé set himself for the kick. But the moment the shot was unleashed the roar began and when the ball settled into the net the crowd went berserk in celebration, the noise level nearly powerful enough to shake nearby buildings. The stadium had been prepared for the moment and in a festive gesture 1,000 balloons were released, all of them stamped with the news that Pelé had scored 1,000 goals. Fireworks were set off. Many fans danced in the aisles of the gigantic stadium. The police and security men that had been hired in abundance to protect Pelé in case he was rushed by fans and overwhelmed forgot themselves and rather than stand as human barricades, they actually joined the celebratory crush.

Almost immediately, Pelé was surrounded by well-wishers and raised on teammates' shoulders. Vasco da Gama players shook his hand. His Santos game jersey was ripped from his chest, but it was promptly replaced with a new, pre-printed jersey that had its own writing on it—"1,000." When it was obvious the ball was safely in the net, Pelé followed it at a sprint, scooped it up, and kissed it. Tears flowed down his face, partly out of joy and appreciation, partly out of relief.

"The pressure was bigger than anything I had ever experienced," Pelé said. "Tonight I shook for the first time." [11]

After the emotional culmination of reaching the 1,000-goal mark, Pelé was removed from the game. Santos won 2–1. In the locker room, Pelé collected his thoughts, dried his tears, and absorbed the sense of relief coursing through his body.

"I slowly took off the new jersey with the number 1,000 on it, folded it neatly and laid it down on the bench beside me to be taken home and treasured forever," he said. [12] The fans had found a way to give the man who had everything a present and souvenir that, until that night, he did not have and had not earned. Now that he had done so, he received a special keepsake to mark the occasion, a game he would never forget either.

A veteran Brazilian sportswriter made an odd comment, though seemingly everyone knew what he meant. He said, "If Pelé hadn't been born a man, he would have been born a ball." [13] It was thought that he meant Pelé had such a kinship with soccer no matter what form it took, he would have been part of the game. Or he comprehended which way balls bounced. Maybe.

Pelé, like all of his fans, would have preferred the climactic goal come on a spectacular move, perhaps his signature bicycle kick, rather than a simple penalty kick. Some felt it almost spoiled the moment. That would be equivalent of dismissing the achievement of a baseball player getting his 3,000th hit on a bunt, or a basketball player setting a record with a free throw. Sometimes, even the greatest of athletes must take in stride what occurs during the middle of a game. They can't always shape history to their exact specifications.

The goal was not the type of goal Pelé would have most wanted, but he said that since he rarely took penalty shots, the play was not as easy for him as some might have believed. ". . . when I tried to take that penalty my legs started to shake because I was so nervous. I didn't want to miss that penalty. Yet, I didn't strike it properly and the goalkeeper got a touch on the ball. But it still went in and I was so thankful. The pressure was so unbearable. Imagine what it was like. Everybody stopped. There was a packed Maracana and they all stopped, they all wanted me to score. Yet later they said it was a penalty and they wanted more. My answer to them all is that Pelé always does things differently. It was as if God wanted all the people to stop and look and take their time to see Pelé score that goal. God had said, 'Let's stop the game and watch Pelé's 1,000th goal.' " [14]

What he did not specifically say and could have is that the only thing worse than making the shot would have been missing the shot. That too would probably have been talked about for a long time, although it would eventually have been eclipsed by whatever type of goal Pelé did score.

For as much time as Pelé had to think about what he would do when the moment of the 1,000th goal became reality, to plan any type of reaction, that all went out the window when the moment came. He was excited, emotional, and grateful. One thing that rarely occurs during an athletic contest happened this day. The sportswriters and radio and TV reporters were allowed onto the field to interview Pelé on the spot rather than waiting for a post-game locker room appearance.

As he had said in other circumstances before, Pelé's first thought annunciated was about the poor children of Brazil. He dedicated the goal to them and said they should not be forgotten. While it was a heartfelt sentiment, consistent with his beliefs, not even Pelé could say why he brought up care of children in the first instance of being asked about the goal. It would have made more sense, he said later, if he had dedicated the goal to his mother Dona Celeste since it was her birthday, but he didn't think of doing that until later in the day.

"But I instantly thought of children," Pelé said. Pelé had harbored a concern about proper education for Brazilian youngsters. A few months earlier, he had interrupted a gang of children trying to steal a car and stopped them. Perhaps it was not the right forum for him to bring up the plight of children in the country, but it did not feel wrong to him even later when he re-examined what he said. The linkage of the 1,000th goal, the culmination of hopes and dreams of a small boy grown out of poverty, seemed perfectly acceptable in his mind to the problems society faced in taking care of its children. "I was criticized a bit . . . people accused me of being a demagogue. Or they thought I was being insincere. I think it is important for people like me to put across messages about education. There will be no future if you don't educate young children. When you look around Brazil and see the inner-city problems we have with the homeless and gangs, they are made up of the kids from back then." [15]

As a more worldly man, the king of soccer had become a philosopher king as well. Pelé had been in the spotlight for 11 years by 1969, marking his breakthrough as the 1958 World Cup. He had led the national team to two World Cup titles and played in a third. In 1970, the year after his 1,000th goal was recorded, Brazil was primed for another World Cup challenge.

Only, Pelé had pledged in 1966 never to compete in the World Cup again. His injury, the management of the team, the way opponents were essentially allowed free rein to assault him on the pitch had all disillusioned him on participating in any future World Cup. He had announced it at the time, soon after returning to Brazil from England, and he had no intention of breaking his word. They had conducted World Cups without Pelé in the past and they could do so again.

NOTES

1. Pelé, *My Life in Pictures* (New York: Simon & Schuster, 2008), p. 50.

2. Ibid.

3. Ibid.

4. Ibid.

5. Ibid.

6. Pelé and Robert L. Fish, *My Life and the Beautiful Game* (New York: Doubleday & Company, 1977), p. 215.

7. Ibid., p. 216.

8. Ibid., p. 217.

9. Ibid.

10. Ibid., p. 218.

11. Joe Marcus, *The World of Pelé* (New York: Mason/Charter, 1976), p. 95.

12. Pelé and Fish, p. 219.

13. Harry Harris, *Pelé: His Life and Times* (New York: Welcome Rain Publishers, 2001), p. 89.

14. Ibid., p. 90.

15. Pelé, p. 52.

Chapter 9

WORLD CUP 1970

After Pele's disheartening experience in the 1966 World Cup, where everything went wrong, he pledged never to return to the international showcase of the sport even if he continued his soccer career long enough for another Cup to roll around.

Well, he did and it did. Leading up to the 1970 World Cup in Mexico, Pelé received the most attention of his life as he pursued his 1,000th career goal. That was enough attention to last anyone for a lifetime. The World Cup soccer tournament is the apex of a player's career, however, when virtually the whole planet turns its eyes to the games.

In 1966, Pelé was unhappy with the manner in which Brazil's team was managed. He was disappointed with the team's play. He was furious about how the games were officiated and that he was hurt again. There was not much to take away in the way of sweet memories. When he said he would not play in the World Cup again, he meant it. He was not just spouting off at the moment. He had played in three World Cup competitions and had helped lead Brazil to two championships. That was good enough for him.

World Cup cycles are very long. Everyone realizes that a four-year interim for a player or a team is an eternity. So many things can happen.

Yet, Pelé never changed his mind or softened his stance. Any time the topic came up, he repeated his thoughts—he had no desire to play in another World Cup tournament and had no plans to do so. This was not much of an issue for three years. There was nothing pressing, no commitments had to be made. It was all conversation.

Pelé continued to excel at the sport and sell the sport everywhere that he and Santos traveled. It was undoubtedly true that other players, the national team selectors, and fans all believed that when the time came to ready the country's team for the World Cup, Pelé would be part of it. No one took his lack of interest seriously. They shrugged off his announced plans to remain a Santos player, not a national team player. He was very consistent. He did not vacillate. But then a day came when preparations began for the 1970 Cup. Invitees to training camp had to be made, rosters firmed up, conditioning began.

No Pelé. As he had said all along, he had no intention of competing in the Cup tournament. Pelé saw no reason to repeat a miserable experience such as the one he endured in 1966, so he continued to say he wasn't playing. Brazilian soccer fans became nervous. For the first time, they started to believe him. Invitations had gone out in 1969 and there was no indication Pelé planned to accept.

Other coaches and players and Brazil soccer administration figures began talking to Pelé, lobbying him to play, piling pressure on him. He felt he had nothing to prove, just didn't want to be involved with the politics of team administration, and most definitely did not want to sign on to play if he thought he wouldn't be able to do his best. If officials were not going to whistle players attacking him, then there was no point, was there?

"There's always somebody gunning for me. I know that the players are ordered to do it," Pelé said of the hits he took, "and I don't hold it against them too much. They have to do their jobs. But the referees aren't doing theirs. I've been pushed, tripped, kicked, every foul there is. If I tried the same things against someone else I'd be thrown out of the game. But other players get away with it against me. What makes me most angry is that the public pays to see me play good football, and then the other teams won't let me."[1]

The debate began for real. The debate raged in public. Some pleaded with Pelé to play. Some wanted the government to order him to play.

By that time, Pelé had made good on his promise not to play internationally. He called it his retirement from international soccer and did not represent Brazil overseas for two years.

While there was considerable external pressure leveraged on Pelé to play this one more time in the World Cup for his country, the swirling discussions did make him re-examine his stand. In the end, several factors contributed to Pelé changing his mind and committing to the 1970 Brazil World Cup team and they were not really based on what soccer fans or others said to him. They more revolved around how he viewed himself.

"Santos was playing well and I was maintaining my role as the leading scorer," Pelé said, "and this filled me with confidence. More importantly I decided I was not going to end my career as a loser. After everything I had achieved, after the buzz of scoring 1,000 goals, I was not going to take my leave from the international game under a cloud. I was going to go out on top. I may have competed in three World Cups already, but in none of them did I take part in every game in the tournament. I was desperate to play a complete tournament. That gave me a lot of focus. I had something to prove. There was also the motivation of national pride."[2]

More so than even other countries that were passionate about soccer, in Brazil, the fans talked the sport, breathed the sport, and allowed it to take over their minds and thoughts. Would Pelé play? Would Pelé sit out? This was the topic of ongoing conversations in the streets, in the barber shops, around dining room tables. For the average Brazilian, it was imperative that Pelé play. He was the identity of Brazilian soccer. Although he had returned a young hero from the 1958 World Cup championship, Pelé had not fared as well in Cup play since.

It was frustrating that Pelé kept getting injured at inconvenient times. That was one reason he was not fulfilled. Certainly, if the 1966 Cup campaign had been more satisfying and Brazil had retired the Jules Rimet Trophy with a third straight championship, it would have been easier for him to graciously step aside and say, "Let the younger players play." Pelé could find reasons for motivation, and although there was no opportunity for a do-over there were a few things that he and Brazil could put right if he played one more time.

"I wanted to put to rest, once and for all, the idea that I couldn't enter a World Cup series without getting hurt," he said.[3]

So when the final selection was made, there was Pelé once again on the Brazilian national team, ready to sweep through Mexico and add the Jules Rimet Trophy to its permanent collection once and for all. If Brazil could win this time, it got to keep the trophy on perpetual display and a new trophy with a different name would be introduced a few years later. Brazil's team promised to be a very strong one. It had the blend of experience and youth and talent. That was encouraging. But there was also an unexpected development that boosted Pelé's morale and pointed him in the right direction to participate. In time for the 1970 Cup, FIFA, the governing body for professional soccer, took a serious look at the way the game was played. Without explicitly saying so, the organization agreed with Pelé. Apparently, it believed the game would be more fun to watch and attract bigger audiences if clubs didn't have to worry so much about its star players getting hurt by opposing teams.

Pelé was correct in complaining about an epidemic of bullies on the field whose sole reason for being on a roster was to hurt other teams' stars. In this respect, at the time, soccer was more like ice hockey. A player dribbling the ball up-field was an open target for defenders much like a hockey player skating up-ice with the puck on his stick had to be stopped at all costs. Contact sports are always seeking to maintain a balance between allowing its stars to operate with freedom and its defenses not to be put in a hopeless situation.

The rule introduced to help the innocent offensive player to survive is a very familiar one to soccer fans who began following the sport over the last 40-plus years. If a player is deemed to be playing too rough or violently, he gets a warning. A referee takes a yellow card out of his pocket and waves it to indicate the player's unsportsmanlike conduct. A yellow card serves as a warning, just as driving along the street, a motorist can be warned that the street light is changing when it turns to yellow. A player who does not heed the threat inherent in a yellow card runs the risk of being thrown out of the game if his poor behavior persists. In that case, the official can escalate matters and pull a red card. The penalty for being hit with a red card is expulsion from the game.

What this indicated to Pelé is that other teams would not be permitted to declare open season on him during the Cup tournament. For Pelé, that was a big issue disposed of. There was also the matter of team selection and preparation. Top leaders in the Brazilian federation were replaced and a new plan for the lead-up to the tournament was instituted. Rather than split up the contenders for the final roster, the entire group of prospective players gathered in one place and stayed in one place for the three months of training camp.

Everything fell into place to relieve Pelé's anxieties, to solve his problems. Once the roots of his dissatisfaction were dealt with, Pelé saw no obstacle to returning to World Cup play to represent Brazil in 1970. There was one major difference compared to recent past Cups. Brazil had to qualify, was not going to be included in the field based on past successes.

Brazil's quest for 1970 World Cup supremacy began on August 6, 1969, when the national team defeated Colombia 2–0, in Bogota. A fresh Brazilian star, Tostao—like Pelé, a goal-scoring specialist—had emerged and as an experiment, they were played together. Tostao scored both goals. That was the first step forward in qualifying. The Brazilians had a few days off for recovery and then met Venezuela in Caracas. Brazil got stronger as this game went on, with Tostao scoring three goals and Pelé two in the 5–0 victory. As Brazil sought to polish off all contenders from South America, Paraguay fell 3–0.

Brazil next had a home game and overpowered Colombia 6–2 in the country's favorite stadium, the Maracana. Tostao and Pelé continued to mesh well, setting each other up for first-rate scoring opportunities. As the entire team came together with a smoothness that was missing in 1966, Pelé's appreciation for coach Joao Saldanha also increased. Saldanha seemed to have a negative history of alienating people with a quick temper, but once he took charge of the national team, he did a superb job of blending players' skills and his lineups. Brazil was talented and Saldanha knew how to deploy his weapons.

Pelé liked the way Saldanha made firm decisions and he obviously had a skill for using the right men in the right combinations. "What a difference from 1966," Pelé said, "when nobody knew until the kickoff who was going to play, and when six or seven changes in the starting lineup were not unknown."[4]

A fresh sense of excitement gripped the country as the new-look World Cup challengers took shape and thoroughly handled every challenger in the region. About 123,000 people came out for a match against Venezuela and Brazil looked brilliant with its 6–0 triumph.

Tostao had three goals on the board with 18 minutes still to go in the first half. Pelé assisted on four goals and nailed two on his own, including the last one. The most energizing moment may have been near the end of the game, when Tostao and Pelé passed the ball back and forth with such crispness, it baffled the defenders and electrified the crowd.

The last element of the job of qualifying was accomplished in a one-goal defeat of Paraguay, with Pelé gaining the game winner, as more than 183,000 fans attended. The most fundamental business—gaining eligibility in the field of 32 for the Cup matches in Mexico—had been taken care of for Brazil. Now, it was a matter of fine-tuning, of staying sharp, of nurturing a team with tremendous potential through the following months before the games between those gathered from all over the world.

During the six qualifying games, Brazil outscored opponents 23–2. Despite that nonstop series of terrific showings, problems began to brew inside the Brazilian operation. All of a sudden, Saldanha, who could do no wrong, reverted to his previous personality traits and began stirring up angry emotions and started pushing all of the wrong buttons. He made player cuts, alienated star players by changing game strategy, and Brazil lost matches to nonqualifying Cup teams. At one point, Saldanha said maybe it was time for Brazil's national team to move on without Pelé. That did not play well with Pelé, the fans, or team officials, who suddenly became quite concerned over the mood of the team.

The situation took on more elements of the bizarre when after being sharply criticized by another Brazilian coach, Saldanha showed up at that man's practice field brandishing a pistol. The matter was defused when the other coach was not present and others at the field confiscated the gun. That was pretty much the last straw for Saldanha, who was fired. Team officials had trouble getting anyone to take the job at first, before turning to Mario Lobo Zagalo, who led the nation to victory in the 1958 and 1962 World Cup competitions.

Yet, the book was not quite closed on Saldanha, who began publicly attacking Pelé and blaming him for his ouster. He spoke to sportswriters and went on television and spread venomous comments about Pelé. He even began dispensing slanderous statements indicating that

Pelé probably had a secret, debilitating disease, and that at 29 he was too old and slowing down to play World Cup soccer. Pelé was alternately furious and concerned that maybe the team discovered something wrong with him during one of its medical exams and was withholding the information from him.

"For a while he had me believing that I was suffering from cancer, or something equally frightening," Pelé said. "Saldanha could not permit himself to leave with no glory, without some justification for being replaced, and he therefore decided to charge me with the responsibility for his fall."[5]

Pelé did have one powerful insider ally in this fiasco who was not scared of speaking out in his defense. Carlos Alberto was not only Santos' captain, but he was the World Cup team captain and had great admiration and affection for Pelé. "Pelé was the player in whom we trusted," Alberto said. "If Pelé is with us, we are with God."[6] God had no comment on this matter, staying out of the dispute, but Saldanha did inject doubts into fans' minds of Pelé's capabilities at this age.

The atmosphere grew more relaxed once Zagalo took control and Saldanha retreated into the background. It took some effort, though, to regain the momentum the team showed in qualifying, when it played superbly every match. Although Brazil stayed in shape by playing some friendlies and winning them, the edge was not there. Pelé, Alberto, and Gerson, the three dominant personalities on the team, met regularly on their own to discuss ideas, strategies, and ways to pull the younger plays back together into a tighter unit. They became known as "the Cobras," as a group within the group. They said they took on this role because Zagalo was coming late to the process, had been away from the national team for a while, and may not known as much about some of the younger players. They became, in essence, a kitchen cabinet, trying to smooth things out again.

This trio presented Zagalo with a proposed lineup change, moving some key personnel around, and the coach liked the sound of it enough to try it out in an exhibition game before departing for Mexico. It involved the sensitive issue of moving Tostao, the great goal-scorer, but Tostao signed off on the suggestion, and the new formation proved to be just what the team needed to reintroduce pizzazz to the offense.

The team loosened up as well, and the players began playing pranks on one another. Even the great Pelé was not off-limits as a victim for these shenanigans. It was known that his greatest fears were snakes and knives. Rivelino was one of the biggest practical jokers on the squad, and one day, he found a wooden snake and put it in Pelé's bed, a joke that would take several hours to play out. After leaving the snake for Pelé to find and before anything happened, Rivelino underwent a crisis of conscience. He started to think he might have made a mistake. He told his roommate what he had done and fretted, "Can you imagine if something happens to him?" He was worried that in his fright Pelé might trip over something and break a bone or tear a muscle. "I will not be able to go back to Brazil." Rivelino had just about talked himself into sneaking back into Pelé's room to retrieve the wooden snake when he heard a scream. Pelé had found the snake and beat on it with his guitar. Later, he discovered who the culprit was.[7] But it was a friendly insult fired back at Rivelino, even if Pelé was not happy about being pranked at the time.

Parts of Mexico are located at an altitude of more than a mile high and Mexico City, the capital, is situated at an altitude of 7,350 feet. When Mexico City hosted the 1968 Summer Olympics, there were numerous comments made about how the high altitude affected athletic performances, especially the distance runners in the track and field. Brazil arrived three weeks before its first game in order to acclimatize to the thinner air.

While one of the complaints Pelé had about the organization of the 1966 team was that the administration took things for granted, this time, the team's back-up support was so detailed, it amazed people. "We took advantage of technological developments," Pelé said. "Our team shirts were re-designed to prevent the collars from accumulating sweat, and each player's kit was made to measure. The research was second-to-none, so sophisticated, in fact, in its detailed analysis of players' physiology that we were mocked in some quarters, presumably for taking things too seriously."[8]

However, as Pelé, noted, there was no such thing as taking soccer too seriously in Brazil. What had diminished somewhat, though, was the sense of optimism that made supporters think of the group as a super team. That sort of giddy optimism had piped down with the coaching transition and all of the bad publicity fomented by Saldanha.

"When we finally went to Mexico there were many, both at home and abroad, who felt Brazil didn't have a chance in the games," Pelé said. "They felt we were insufficiently trained, that the disagreements that had led to a change in our coaching staff, even though resolved, had led to dissension that would be difficult to overcome."[9]

By that time, that was all less worrisome than Tostao's health. He had suffered a detached retina in 1968 after a ball struck him hard in the eye. But he had been fine for many months afterward. Then, it was suddenly announced that he had to return to a hospital in Houston, Texas, for additional treatment. Pelé worried that Tostao, who took it easy on headers now, might be a bit psyched out.

Another new element in team preparation for the games was daily group prayer. Although players were of different religions, not all Roman Catholics as Pelé was, they found common ground in something just about every night after dinner, though no one was forced to participate. "We found something to pray for every day—the sick, the war in Vietnam, the health of someone who needed our prayers, all sorts of things," Pelé said.[10]

In preliminary play, Brazil was grouped with defending champion England, Czechoslovakia, and Romania. Brazil topped the Czechs 4–1, and Pelé learned from studying tapes that Czechoslovakia's net-minder Viktor had a tendency to wander far from the goal mouth when the ball was at the other end of the field. In one game Pelé was guiding the ball in his own territory and was starting to dribble up-field slowly. Thinking of the old game tapes, Pelé spotted Viktor a bit out of position, and then reared back, and boomed a long kick. Pelé said if the ball had gone into the net, it would have been one of the most memorable shots of his career.

Brazil finished first, going 3–0, with eight goals for and three against. England won two of its games and tied another. Brazil defeated England 1–0. The contest against England was viewed as a match between two soccer powers with contrasting approaches. England relied on cautionary defense and Brazil thrived in the wide-open game. The lone goal came from Jairzinho on an assist from Pelé.

On June 14, playing the quarterfinals in Guadalajara, Brazil prevailed over Peru 4–2.

The Peru coach was Didi, the former Pelé teammate on the earlier World Cup champion teams. Most of the crowd was backing Peru because the country had recently endured a disastrous earthquake. The magnitude 7.9 quake had killed at least 100,000 people and injured another 200,000 people. "We sympathized with the Peruvians, too," Pelé said, "but that did not mean we could afford to lose to them."[11]

Elsewhere that day, the tough English squad lost its chance to repeat when West Germany knocked them out of the tournament by a 3–2 score. Uruguay topped the Soviet Union 1–0, to advance to a semifinals match against Brazil. There were only three days to prepare for the June 17 next round, and although Brazil had a familiarity with Uruguay since the teams were from the same region of the world, the squads had not met in a game for 20 years.

The last meeting, on July 16, 1950, had been a bitter one. That year, Brazil was chosen to host the World Cup and the Maracana Stadium was built to hold nearly 200,000 fans. Whether in attendance or listening to the radio, the entire Brazilian nation, it seemed, was paying attention to the game. The hunger was there to capture the country's first World Cup championship. Brazil had the superior forces and even before the game kicked off versus Uruguay, some people were planning a celebration.

Pelé was nine years old, just shy of his 10th birthday and he and family members had the radio going in their home waiting for Brazil, which was in its first finals game, trying to win its first Cup title. Brazil took a 1–0 lead and everyone at Pelé's house was screaming in reaction. The fans in the streets shouted, as did the announcer on the radio. Uruguay came back to knot the game at 1–1, but that wasn't so bad because under the rules in effect at the time from its previous results, all Brazil needed was a tie for the victory. But then, late in the game, Uruguay pumped home another goal for a 2–1 lead and that lead held up. Uruguay, not Brazil, became World Cup champion on Brazilian soil.

"It is a day I shall never forget," Pelé said more than a quarter of a century after that game was played. "I shall never feel (it) duplicated. It is as if Brazil had lost a war in which they were in the right, and not only lost it, but lost it with ignominy and many dead. The general grief is inconsolable. I cry and I cannot stop myself, but I am not the only one crying."[12]

There was no party to attend. There was no dancing in the street. Everyone stayed home to mourn the defeat, but as Pelé put it, Brazilian soccer fans never forgot the loss. Pelé was old enough to remember 1950 in 1970, but not all of his teammates were. Some of them were just 22. It was the players who were on the older side who knew the story of Brazil–Uruguay that were most excited about this match. It was a chance to avenge their elders of a generation before. This was a chance that might never come again—another critical World Cup game between the same nations.

It didn't matter so much if the younger Brazilian players did not know the history because the night before this game, they were all reminded. Pelé remembers fans trooping to the team hotel with such purpose. The players were actually told that it would not hurt so much if they did not win the title, but that above all, these younger Brazilians had to beat Uruguay to avenge the honor of the earlier team. For their side, Uruguayan fans with long memories not only took heart from the previous victory, but actually taunted Brazilian fans over it. That galled the Brazilians no end.

"They've been a bone stuck in our throats for 20 long years and you have to get them out of there," Pelé and his playing partners were told. Again and again, such messages of exhortation were delivered to the players in the days leading up to the semifinal. "They're going around telling people that just the sight of the Uruguayan uniform is enough to make all Brazilians tremble in their boots—that you are so afraid of them that only the police will be able to get you onto the field at all. You have to make them eat those words."[13]

Those civilians, so to speak, relayed these insults to their favorite players one by one, urging them to do something about it. The players were reminded they were playing for pride, for the honor of their insulted country. There were many circumstances that made this game one of the most important in Brazilian soccer history. There was the presence of Pelé, the world's greatest player, almost assuredly for the last time in Cup play. Brazil's psyche needed the boost it would receive from cleansing the slate with Uruguay. The players were beginning to believe they were the best soccer squad ever assembled, but they had to win the World Cup to prove that.

Brazil was brimming with emotion and motivation, with a feeling of anticipation, obligation, and a desire for victory. Then, Uruguay came out and scored the first goal for a 1–0 lead. That was not part of the game plan. Minutes passed and the end of the 45-minute first half approached. Tostao issued a long pass to Clodoaldo that caught the Uruguayan defense napping. The ball sailed over the defenders' heads and Clodoaldo scooped up the ball, burst in on the Uruguayan goalie, and fired on the net. Goooaaaalllll!

Despite all of those reasons to be hungry, Brazil had actually played a bit flat in the first half to fall behind. In the locker room at halftime, the Brazilians discussed what they could do to disrupt Uruguay's style. The plan Zagalo outlined was for the Brazilians to come out attacking, stay aggressive, and keep attacking. It worked. Jairzinho and Rivelino scored goals to make the lead 3–1, and that's where it stayed.

Brazil's victory over Uruguay transcended a championship tournament. In terms of importance in Brazil and shaping memories, this soccer game is comparable to the United States' Winter Olympic gold-medal winning hockey game of 1980 in Lake Placid, New York. Winning the gold medal was a spectacular feat, and one that is etched in memory among American fans. However, the game that is best remembered from that tournament is the U.S. semifinal victory over the Soviet Union. Many people forget that the monumental upset did not occur in the championship game. Likewise, all this game against Uruguay accomplished was moving ahead. Once Brazil dispatched Uruguay, Brazil still had to play someone else for the Cup crown. The challenge was rechanneling energy and focus so as to stay sky high for the final game, as it turned out to be, against Italy.

Brazil met Italy on June 21, 1970, in the Azteca Stadium of Mexico City in front of more than 107,000 fans. If Brazil could win the game, it would capture its third World Cup since 1958 and the trophy would travel to Brazil for good, not remain on display at FIFA headquarters. It was a very hot and muggy night. Physically, Brazil was in good shape, with no major injuries. Mentally, Brazil was psyched to win and had a lot going for it. One thing the players could have done without is the pressure they felt to win. "The final is everything," Pelé said, quickly putting Uruguay on the shelf. "It is for the championship. And the championship is all that counts."[14]

Pelé scored the first goal and the Brazilians never trailed. Gerson, Jairzinho, and Carlos Alberto scored the goals in a 4–1 Brazilian victory. The Cup was headed back to Brazil, this time to stay. The Jules

Rimet trophy would reside in Brazil for good. This was one of the greatest triumphs in Brazilian soccer history. Pelé had become the first player to be part of three Cup-winning teams.

As the years passed and technology was improved and spread, sitting back home and listening to the big game on radio was no longer the thing to do. No, the thing to do now was to sit back home and watch the big game on television. The world was watching when Brazil claimed the trophy. Inside the stadium, a large percentage of the fans were rooting for Brazil. When the game ended and the score was final, the Brazilian players ran around on the field hugging one another, though that was only a mini part of the celebration. Fans came pouring out of the stands to do some hugging of their own and to scarf up some kind of World Cup souvenir.

These were the most vociferous and energetic fans, ones that didn't care about dodging security policemen in their attempts to salvage something. These were not the kind of fans that paused at the souvenir booths to buy T-shirts or World Cup pins, but who acted as if they were alcohol-fueled. While Pelé sought to share the moment with his friends and teammates, the more aggressive soccer fans flooded the field and mobbed Pelé. By the time they got done stripping him of his uniform parts, Pelé was wearing just his tight underwear shorts and he was worried he might lose that small garment that protected the last bits of his dignity.

With the grand accomplishment in Mexico City achieved as the entire world watched, a happy but exhausted Pelé walked off the pitch content. Soon after the team returned home, Pelé began thinking about retirement from the sport he so loved and which sustained him.

Pelé had played on three World Cup winners. He had scored 1,000 goals and he was part of the squad that gained revenge on Uruguay. He had made more money than he had ever dreamed of earning and accumulating. It was not long before he informed Brazilian authorities that they should no longer consider him for selection to the national team when international matches came along. He also informed Santos that it might begin looking for a replacement to wear the number 10 jersey for the club.

Pelé knew that he could keep playing for quite a while, but he was turning 30, had an infant son in the family joining his daughter Kelly

Cristina and thought it was time to spend more time at home with Rosemeri and cease touring the world. Pelé envisioned his departure from the game as a slow-motion retirement, taking it one step at a time, not retiring cold turkey right after this fulfilling victory.

NOTES

1. Pete Axthelm, "The Most Famous Athlete in the World," *Sports Illustrated*, October 24, 1966.

2. Pelé, *My Life in Pictures* (New York: Simon & Schuster, 2008), p. 55.

3. Harry Harris, *Pelé: His Life and Times* (New York: Welcome Rain Publishers, 2001), p. 92.

4. Ibid., p. 94.

5. Ibid., p. 97.

6. Ibid.

7. Ibid., p. 100.

8. Pelé, p. 55.

9. Pelé and Robert L. Fish, *My Life and the Beautiful Game* (New York: Doubleday & Company, 1977), p. 224.

10. Pelé, pp. 55–56.

11. Pelé and Fish, p. 235.

12. Ibid., p. 240.

13. Ibid., p. 242.

14. Ibid., p. 245.

Chapter 10

EASING INTO RETIREMENT

Winning the World Cup trophy in 1970 was a special gift to the Brazilian people. It was almost too good to be true, the foremost soccer lovers in the world felt. One event that has made Brazil famous is the annual carnival in Rio each February. It is regarded as one of the world's grandest and wildest parties. Yet, the spontaneous victory celebration serving as a coronation for the Brazilian soccer champs likely even eclipsed that volume of participants.

Between Rio de Janeiro and Sao Paulo, millions of people poured into the streets to sing, dance and shout, to share their happiness over the World Cup triumph. They also lit off fireworks, hugged their neighbors, made noise with horns and sirens and anyone who was behind the wheel of a car put his hand on the horn and left it there.

In Mexico, Pelé was so overcome by the results and the victory that he slipped away from his teammates for a short while at their hotel, even as the team party was beginning and the Brazilian journalists accompanied the team. He briefly retreated to his hotel room to offer a prayer of thanks, and by the time he rejoined the team, he had missed some of the official photographs. That night, the Brazilian team was feted with a banquet and a show until 1:00 A.M.—indoors. Outside, the party went on all night.

As soon as the result registered, prominent Brazilians began sending telegrams of congratulations to the hotel and President Emilio Medici telephoned and spoke to Pelé, Carlos Alberto, and a few other members of the squad, offering his own comments. The main miracle of the day was that the president was able to get through because of the number of incoming calls to the team at the hotel and the number of outgoing calls from journalists to their affiliations.

Before returning home, Pelé demonstrated how he had seemingly become wiser over the years upon the realization that fans can love a player to death. Unlike the time he was virtually stripped of his clothing after the 1,000th goal, as soon as the game with Italy ended, Pelé took his own shirt off. He considered it a self-protective measure.

"I had no intention of being strangled by some delirious fan," he said. That gesture didn't save his boots or shorts, however. Back in the locker room, Pelé retreated to the team showers to take time out for a little prayer to thank God for all the good fortune in his life. Yet, he barely had a moment of privacy. The sportswriters covering the game demanded his presence and attention and barged fully clothed into the shower to ask him questions. [1]

Naturally, when the team returned home, it was feted to an unbelievable extent, starting with a motorcade from the airport to downtown Rio. The players were not sheltered, either, but displayed on the backs of trucks, all waving to their adoring public. Then, much of the same was repeated on a visit to Sao Paulo.

Three World Cup championships were enough for Pelé. He knew that his journey to the title in Mexico City was going to be his farewell to Cup competition. He was pretty sure of that in 1966, but was glad he came back for one more go-around in the world's largest soccer tournament.

As a member of the 1958, 1962, and 1970 Brazil World Cup championship teams, Pelé was unique. If anything illustrated how difficult it was to keep playing at the highest level of the sport year after year, it was the fact that Pelé was now the only man who had played for three Cup champions. That spanned 12 years. He had also played for a nonwinning Brazilian team, gaining a coveted roster spot four times.

Making the team alone so often was an achievement. It reflected the fact that he was selected for his first World Cup team as a

17-year-old—a precocious age for an international player. Now Pelé was going to be 30, and while he was physically strong enough to continue at the top level of the game for a couple of additional years, he did not want to put the strain on his body by adding thousands and thousands of flight miles and he said he did not want to spend as much time away from home.

Santos, Pelé's club team in Brazil, had benefited handsomely from his services. It had become one of the most famous teams in the world and when other top teams in other nations wanted to schedule matches that would draw fans, they thought of Santos first, provided Pelé was along for the ride. It was even written into contracts that in games against Santos, if Pelé could not play, the Brazilian club's share of the gate receipts would be smaller.

Pelé was grateful to Santos as well. The team had been good to him from the time he was a teenager and his identification with the club had brought him fame and fortune. Immediately following the 1970 World Cup, Pelé had made his intentions clear to the national team. He was done representing the country in international play. He planned to play another season or two with Santos and then retire altogether from active play in the sport that had been his profession and love.

Pelé had always valued his father, Dondinho's counsel and he remembered him saying long ago that he should not stay too long, but rather recognize when his body began to fail him and step away from the limelight before someone else in authority asked him to do so. That was what was on Pelé's mind following the World Cup championship because he did feel fine and did feel he could play top-notch soccer for the next couple of years.

"And I was absolutely at the top," Pelé said. "I had played my best World Cup, scored 1,000 goals, and was an international name. I was in no hurry to leave, but it was important to me to indicate my long-term intentions."[2]

Pelé's son, Edson Cholby do Nascimento, was born two months after the World Cup of 1970. He would be too young to remember much about his father's playing career. Pelé's retirement from soccer was a long-term plan. His first announcement was declaring that he would play in no more World Cup tournaments. That was an easy one to make because the last one was so recent and fresh in people's minds and it would be four years before the next tournament took place.

"It was not a matter of age or physical condition," Pelé said, "my condition was excellent, as evidenced by my performances in the 1970 games, and, as for my age, in 1974 I would still be only 33 years old. I wanted to leave the national team when I was fit and in good enough condition to continue if I had wanted to. I didn't want to wait until the fans were booing me off the pitch."[3]

Pelé was a long way from being booed because of the deterioration of his talents. Later, he revealed a more disturbing reason for his withdrawal from the national team, a powerful indicator of his maturity and his thinking at the time, and yet, something no one suspected because he always tried to stay politically neutral.

As a youngster, when he was first learning the basics of the game and throwing himself into local soccer play with friends on the street, Pelé did not care much about anything beyond the sport that enraptured him. He disliked school and didn't study because of one particular teacher and he dropped out at a very early age because of conflict. He much later gained a high school equivalency diploma, though he also kept that secret for a long time.

By the time Pelé was in his mid-teens, he was living away from home, linked to Santos, and playing soccer as a profession with older, adult men. He had a limited childhood and a very short period of time where he led a normal teenaged life. Very quickly, he became famous, then rich, then more famous and richer still. He was the best-known athlete in the world and pretty much the best-known human being. He was considered to be a veritable god among his Brazilian fans, and yet, worked very hard to relate to the common man and not put on airs or pretensions. He expressed no ambition to run for political office. For the most part, Pelé stayed humble and religious and was closely identified as a family man, not a swinger who went nightclubbing.

Most often, when he traveled, chiefs of state sought out Pelé, not vice-versa. They, like the average fan, were fascinated by his play and wanted to meet and touch the man. It was not generally part of Pelé's makeup to schmooze with other celebrities, but he was always willing to lend his name to charitable causes, took great pride in representing the Brazilian people in international sports, and was certainly the nation's finest ambassador. As a national treasure, he was not a true export, but wherever Pelé played and displayed his game, he made friends for his country.

As innately wise as Pelé seemed to be in his dealings with most individuals, he was not terribly politically savvy about the truth about what was happening in his own land. He was no politician and worked hard to stay clear of controversial issues. Therefore, it was with dismay that he began to comprehend some of the negative things propagated by the military government that ran Brazil.

In 1964, the Brazilian military led a coup against the civilian, elected government and overthrew it because of the suggestion it was communist-influenced. Between that March and March 1985, various groups vied for control of the country, from rebels to unhappy student demonstrators, to military leaders. But the military held sway.

One reason that Pelé wished to back away from the national team after the 1970 World Cup was because it symbolized connection to the government, though that was not something he said aloud at the time. "I was beginning to learn some of the truth about what was going on in my country," Pelé said, "the torture, the killings, the disappeared. I didn't want to pull on a Brazilian shirt while the military were running the country."[4]

And so began what Pelé intended to be a gradual withdrawal from the soccer spotlight. In mid-July 1971—a year after the World Cup championship—Pelé engaged in two international matches while wearing the national team colors inside Brazil. On July 11, he competed in Sao Paulo versus Austria. That day, Pelé played just the first half or 45 minutes and he did score a goal. That was his final goal tallied representing Brazil internationally, the 77th in all, a national record that has lasted.

A week later, on July 18, in an event that was advertised as Pelé's farewell to the international sport, he pulled on his number 10 jersey for his country for the last time. Brazil met Yugoslavia and some 180,000 fans turned out. Of course, Pelé said, this last game of this sort had to be played in the Maracana Stadium.

"It was not the best game of my career," Pelé said. "I was too emotionally involved knowing I would never again wear the yellow and green colors of Brazil on the football field. Nor did it help my concentration to have 180,000 fans standing and shouting in rhythmic

It was a very emotional time for Pelé when he chose to retire from representing Brazil in international competition and then played his final game for his favorite club team, Santos. Little did he and his fans realize it was only a temporary retirement and that Pelé would soon return to play a few seasons for the New York Cosmos in the United States. (AP Photo/Matias Rezende/Gervasio Baptista)

unison: 'Fica! Fica!' meaning 'Stay! Stay!' " It is likely that even years later Pelé can still hear that chant ringing in his ears. It is not something an athlete ever forgets. "It was an intensely emotional moment for me."[5]

In a unique sort of tribute, in Seville, Spain, the day's bullfights were called off so sports fans could stay at home to watch Pelé's last international game on live television. The game was big business for Rio, and not just from ticket sales. Brazilian fans traveled from the far reaches of the country to attend and filled all of the hotel rooms. Street vendors stockpiled a department store's-worth of Pelé souvenirs and sold out. About this time, the government had authorized the printing of a postage stamp with Pelé on it and some kiosk sellers were selling posters with the same picture on it. There was definitely Pelé mania in Rio.

At the end of the game, which had a final score of 2–2, Pelé ran what might be termed a career victory lap, circling the stadium as the thunderous chant resumed, again calling for him to change his mind and stay with the national team. Pelé peeled off his shirt with the number 10 on it, and waved it above his head as he held his arms in the air. Then, he used the cloth article to wipe tears from his face. He displayed the jersey to the crowd, but could not control his own crying at that point. When the event was over, he said he would never forget that day.

Another major reason Pelé dropped his national team responsibilities was because of the amount of travel involved. Although sometimes countries sent teams to Brazil, more often than not, he was traveling to other lands to play. He wanted to be closer to his family, had begun taking university classes to follow his high school equivalency diploma, and he wanted to spend more time behind his desk managing his businesses and finances.

"I had enough travel to last me several lifetimes," Pelé said. "I was tired of living in airplanes and out of suitcases. I had decided to return to school for a very good reason. During the playing season I was often called upon to speak at various universities or high schools, or even hospitals, telling those who attended these lectures all about football, its history, its skills, my travels, and anything else they cared to question me about."[6]

On many of those appearances, Pelé brought along his good friend Julio Mazzei, who had morphed from the Santos' trainer into Pelé confidante, advisor, and godfather of his son. When he couldn't answer a question, Pelé asked Mazzei to do it for him. Painfully aware that he lacked enough formal education, Pelé did not enjoy being put in that situation. So, that helped inspire him to begin taking college classes upon his national team retirement. In addition, Mazzei, his wife Rosemeri, and his brother, who was then in law school, all encouraged him along those lines.

After a lifetime defined by soccer, Pelé had to begin investigating what to do with the rest of his life. He was just turning 31 in 1971.

However, even after the grand finale with the national team, Pelé remained under contract with Santos. That deal did not expire until the end of 1972 and he planned to fulfill it. While Santos often played home games, eliminating the need for travel for many league contests, the club was still very much in demand for appearances around the world and that had a lot to do with Pelé. That meant he was still on the go to foreign lands. Now, though, the soccer fans in those places recognized that this was probably going to be the last time they saw him display his skills in person, bringing out even bigger crowds.

At about this same time in 1972, the family moved into a new house designed and built with input from Rosemeri and Pelé. It was very secure and somewhat secluded so that Pelé could retain his privacy. By then, he owned a Mercedes automobile with a license plate that read "1000" to commemorate his achievement scoring the 1,000 goals.

There was only one problem. Between the easily recognizable license plate and the flashy car itself, Pelé had no anonymity when driving. He said he was often pursued for autographs when making the rounds in the Mercedes, so instead when running errands, he often picked people up in his Volkswagen.

While Pelé was preoccupied with disengaging from his soccer commitments, though still traveling on tours with Santos, he had a stopover in Jamaica for an exhibition game. During his time there, he was sought for an appointment by a former British soccer writer named Clive Toye, who had just helped create the New York Cosmos for a fledgling American soccer league. He boldly suggested that Pelé make the jump to New York after he retired from Santos to help build soccer interest in the United States. Pelé did not have the slightest interest in doing so in 1971 and did not envision that such a day would come. However, at the end of their meeting, Toye told Pelé, "Remember the Cosmos, we'll be back when you leave Santos."

Whether that was just a throwaway line or Toye was dead serious about the comment, anyone who knew the history of professional soccer in the United States (almost none) at that time and the history of those who jump-started new professional sports leagues from start (spotty, at best) might not have been willing to bet that the North American Soccer League would still be around when Pelé retired from Santos. [7]

Pelé was most certainly not looking for a new team at the time, nor did he ever believe he would be. He was working to divest himself of the teams he was affiliated with and looking ahead to a life when he might spend all of his footwear shopping time invested in purchasing black dress shoes or sneakers. When considering future careers, there was no time that Pelé expressed the slightest interest in coaching a club team or Brazil's national team. He had no desire whatsoever to coach adults. He did have an interest in teaching children the game of soccer, but the topic of big-time coaching as a way to stay in the game did not attract him.

It would not be unfair to say that Santos booked as many games as possible, in as many places as possible, during the final years it had Pelé under contract. In 1973, Santos played in Australia, the Persian Gulf, Egypt, the Sudan, Germany, France, Belgium, England, and in the United States.

In Gabon, it was said that a minister there who was involved in the payment of fees to Santos for an exhibition game would not fork over the money to anyone except Pelé "because he wanted to have a private conversation with him in his office." King Faisal of Saudi Arabia tried to hire Pelé on the spot to provide soccer demonstrations for children for an entire year for a signing bonus of $400,000 and a salary of $30,000 a month. Feeling awkward, Pelé thanked the king kindly, but said he was bound by his Santos contract and couldn't make it. [8]

Many of the stopovers were exciting and emotional for Pelé because he was honored so many times. During the breadth of his soccer career, Pelé had not visited France nearly as often as some other countries, but on this swing, the French practically adopted him. He met with President Charles De Gaulle and received several presents, including a jewelry case. His hosts threw Pelé a parade in Paris, he rode on a car and it was estimated that 200,000 people turned out to cheer him along the route, which ran through the Arc de Triomphe, a special tribute.

"It is most difficult to express how I felt at the moment," Pelé said. "I know what a parade through the Arc signifies. There have been many war heroes and national heroes so honored and now they have honored me with a similar parade. It is such a great tribute and I am very, very proud. I hope to one day be worthy of such an honor." [9]

Pelé and Santos kept piling up the miles, playing matches against a Bologna, Italy, club on the go in Toronto and New Jersey. Then, when he arrived in New York, men laboring at Kennedy Airport surrounded him and welcomed him spontaneously, acting as if they just had been soccer fans awaiting him with their autograph books. There was an intriguing development in New York when the city would not allow the Bologna–Santos game to be held in Shea Stadium even though the Mets were not playing baseball that day. The game was scheduled for Roosevelt Stadium in Jersey City, an old minor league baseball stadium that seated 24,000 and was later torn down in 1985.

What transpired supported the notion that New York City had made a mistake in not renting out Shea. Fans piled in their cars by the thousands to make the short pilgrimage to New Jersey for the game, creating an epic traffic jam even by Manhattan standards. When game time approached and fans were still stuck in traffic, they simply abandoned their cars at the side of the road and walked to the stadium. The crowd was standing room only, over capacity. Pelé provided an assist on Santos' only goal in a 1–1 game.

Santos and Pelé had another trip to New York, but this time the club engaged a Colombian rival team as part of a doubleheader at Yankee Stadium where the Cosmos also competed.

While originally Pelé intended to wrap up his Santos career earlier, he ended up extending his involvement with the team through 1974. The fact that he was still an active player when the selection arose for the 1974 Brazilian World Cup team thrust his name back into the mix. Pelé had not played for the national team for more than two years, and remained adamant that he was not going to suit up again on the international stage. The pressure started mounting on Pelé in October of 1973 and it was virtually nonstop with pleas to sign up for the West German Cup tournament. Fans wanted him to play one more round. Officials asked him to play. Former President Medici requested that he play. New President Ernesto Geisel urged him to play. Medici even gathered a group of high ranking officials and they trooped to Pelé's office to make an appeal. Still, he said no.

However, given that he was in good condition and was still playing for Santos even though he had not expected to still be around, Pelé did experience a brief moment when he wavered. For a moment, he actually thought he might give in and try to play in the 1974 Cup. But a shocking incident occurred and that firmed up his resolve. Some fans fired two gunshots at his home. That tore it. "I was very bitter about that incident," Pelé said. "I couldn't believe that people would be so upset, when I had only reaffirmed the decision I gave to them three years earlier. It left some bitterness in me. They were never caught, but even if they had been I don't think that I would hold any great grudge against them." [10]

Originally, Pelé was contracted to handle radio and television commentary in Brazil for the 1974 World Cup, but the deal faded away, much to his consternation and he never got an explanation. He traveled to West Germany for the games, anyway. He was given a rousing welcome from the fans, sometimes mobbed. Among the world luminaries that he hobnobbed with besides former soccer stars were American Secretary of State Henry Kissinger, Princess Grace of Monaco, and German Chancellor Helmut Schmidt. Kissinger and Pelé became fairly friendly and in one picture they posed for together, they are smiling like family members displaying joy at a reunion.

Brazil finished fourth in the Cup tournament. For those inclined to blame Pelé for the lower result because of his absence, he was not the only star from four years before who was not participating. The team was pretty much just going through an evolution.

Whether he was naïve, being disingenuous, or exactly what, following the World Cup as his tenure with Santos was nearing an end, Pelé explained what he saw his life being like in the future. "I am about to become Mr. Edson Arantes do Nascimento," he said, "an industrialist, an average father, and a husband. This is my ambition and nothing will change my mind right now. I am just happy I can sign Pelé instead of my full name because I don't think my fingers would be able to take the strain of signing all the autographs I sign using my whole name. My idea is to eventually become just another person to be able to go places without being bothered by autograph hounds." [11]

If that day ever did come, it would be a surprise to those who follow the sports memorabilia market. Of course, when Pelé uttered that comment, it was in the 1970s, and there was no such thing as a sports memorabilia market where collectors spend large sums of money to obtain not only autographed items, but equipment that their sports heroes once wore. Approximately 35 years after Pelé made that statement, he could go access the Internet (which also didn't exist) on a computer (which barely existed) and type in his name in search of his own autograph. He would find a Pelé-signed jersey for sale for more than $1,000, a framed photograph of him taking his famed bicycle kick shot, also autographed and with some Pelé trading cards inserted into the frame for $1,200, and numerous other items. He may or may not remember ever signing the items.

What Pelé was unaware of is that his fame would not really abate, even after he stopped playing soccer professionally and after years passed. The calendar pages turned, and eventually, Pelé's contract with Santos began running down to its final days. Fans found it difficult to get used to the idea of Pelé not playing for the national team in the World Cup. But now, they were going to lose him altogether. Very soon, there would be no more Pelé games to witness of any type. The end process of his staged withdrawal was nigh.

When Pelé signed his final contract with Santos, his periodic hassle with sportswriters reared up. It was reported that he was making outrageous demands. He later called some of the stories "libelous." He also noted, without trying to sound boastful, that he had pretty much made Santos financially sound. "During my time with the club Santos had banked $20 million," Pelé said, "and I don't think it is big-headed to say that a fair proportion of that had come because of me. It is also worth pointing out that in the years after I left Santos didn't play a single game overseas." [12]

Pelé's first contact with Santos dated to 1956. His final obligation as a player culminated in 1974. It was well-known during the 1974 season that Pelé was in his last year with Santos and as the season advanced into autumn, everywhere he played, sellouts followed. One reason for that was because Santos kept hinting that each game would be his last, though it wasn't. The team was chasing the dollars to the very end. It was going to be up to Pelé to choose the precise moment of his departure.

Finally, it was announced that the last game of Pelé's career would take place on October 2 against the Ponte Preta club. Somewhat surprisingly, the game was not shifted to Maracana Stadium, but was played in the much smaller Santos venue at home.

Pelé was somewhat restless the night before the game. He played with his children and talked to his wife and paced in his garage, which held four cars, the splashy Mercedes and three others that were really foreign economy cars that one would not suspect a world famous figure to be driving. He had developed a creative routine to avoid traffic to the stadium. In the Santos locker room, some of Pelé's teammates had tears in their eyes. They recognized they were going to be a piece of history and that they were witnessing the end of an era.

Entering that game, the man of 1,000 goals had actually become the man with 1,220 goals—he had run up the total somewhat since the milestone.

The game began like any other, but after about 20 minutes of play, Pelé caught the ball in his hands and then ran with it to mid-field. Initially, the crowd was stunned into silence. Players did not handle the ball in big-time soccer with their hands. Never. It was against the rules and so ingrained that fans never saw it happen with a player such as

Pelé. He did it for shock value and it worked. The players on the pitch stopped what they were doing to stare at him, as well.

There, Pelé planted the ball on the turf in a dramatic gesture and he dropped to the ground, the ball between his knees. He raised his arms to the fans on each side of the stadium, turning his body, and let the tears roll down his cheeks. This truly was the end. Fans rose to provide a standing ovation. Pelé rose to his feet and ran a lap around the stadium. He ran down the exit tunnel to the Santos locker room alone and entered the dressing room to shed his emotions. However, a photographer for a Sao Paulo newspaper had stayed behind in the locker room, hiding in the showers. When Pelé quietly sat down, dwelling on his thoughts and letting his tears carry him till spent, the photographer snapped a picture that became famous in Brazil.

Pelé dressed in street clothes and left the stadium before the game ended. He could still hear the crowd in the distance as he drove away. He was 33 years old—his 34th birthday beckoned in a couple of weeks. His soccer playing career was over.

"It was hard to believe, but it was true," he said. "I was no longer Pelé. Now I was Edson Arantes do Nascimento once again, and now for all times. And I honestly thought at the time I was telling the truth." [13]

That was the simple man speaking within. Pelé did not realize it, but he would always be Pelé and never Edson again.

NOTES

1. Harry Harris, *Pelé: His Life and Times* (New York: Welcome Rain Publishers, 2001), p. 123.

2. Pelé, *My Life in Pictures* (New York: Simon & Schuster, 2008), p. 64.

3. Harris, pp. 127–128.

4. Ibid., p. 128.

5. Pelé and Robert L. Fish, *My Life and the Beautiful Game* (New York: Doubleday & Company, 1977), pp. 263–264.

6. Ibid., p. 256.

7. Joe Marcus, *The World of Pelé* (New York: Mason/Charter, 1976), p. 116.

8. François Thebaud, *Pele* (New York: Harper & Row Publishers, 1976), p. 117.

9. Marcus, p. 117.

10. Ibid., p. 136.

11. Ibid., p. 139.

12. Pelé, p. 66.

13. Pelé and Fish, p. 282.

Chapter 11

GENTLEMAN BUSINESSMAN

Before Pelé even retired from Santos, he had a major new endorsement deal in place that not only paid him well, but provided him
with an avenue to continue working and expanding his work with
children.

The Pepsi-Cola Company offered Pelé a contract to travel around
the world, teaching soccer to children. He laughingly said "quite unlike
other sponsors (they) did not want me to say I drank their product and
loved it."[1] The soft drink company was the first of any kind of corporate
entity that came to Pelé and offered to underwrite a mission that was
close to his heart. A one-year pact was signed as a getting-to-know-you
measure—on both sides. As a package, Pepsi also signed Julio Mazzei
and the two compadres could travel together, giving seminars.

Somehow, Pelé made this work despite still playing for Santos, taking his college classes, and trying to spend more time with his own family. Pelé may have been a loving husband and father, but he was never
going to be a stay-at-home dad, hands-on raising the kids, and sticking
around nine-to-five. His travels still had him flying all over the world
for Santos or Pepsi now.

Things went so well with Pepsi that after the year was up, a new, five-year contract was put into place. Retiring from Santos cut way, way back on Pelé's time commitments after that year and much of that time was filled representing Pepsi. The Pepsi deal was also a bridge from the end of Pelé's playing days into his new life as a businessman and public figure emeritus.

Before 1971 ended, Pelé had set up his own business headquarters in an office in Santos. He also parted ways with his longtime agent, Marby Ramundini. Pelé had no complaints with the services provided, but felt that not being a full-time player he could now manage his own affairs. They remained friends, just not partners.

Pelé created a new company called the Pelé Administration and Advertising Company. His main financial advisor at first was his Uncle Jorge. Pelé's hands were very much involved with all sectors of the economy, most of them far removed from soccer. He owned real estate in Sao Paulo, Rio, Bauru, and Three Hearts. His properties included houses, stores, and vacant land. He owned a dairy farm, a trucking company, an import-export business, part of a radio station, and more commercial entities. This was in addition to his home and a country ranch.

His portfolio was even wider than that in reality. There was a Pelé Rubber Bands division and his company sold bicycles, toys, razor blades, and transistor radio batteries. There was a time in his life when Pelé could not afford shoes—now, he sold them. He grew up poor, with a limited wardrobe. Now, he could afford the best threads and enjoyed wearing them. Pelé also actually modeled clothing from Pelé Clothes. He got a kick out of displaying the fancier suits.

Holdings outgrew Uncle Jorge's capabilities. Things were getting tangled—something Pelé had always worried about since his earlier-in-life losses. Pelé brought in a more expert financial manager with the orders to straighten everything out. "Heaven may have known what I was involved in," Pelé said. "I didn't."[2]

First, Pelé's new financial manager suggested that he divest himself of small items, investments that were losers, and some investments that produced small returns. The streamlining strengthened Pelé's overall financial position, but the new man, Jose Roberto Ribeiro Xisto, ran into a roadblock with one holding. It was called Fiolax.

Early in his career, Pelé's finances had degenerated and left him in a precarious financial position. Santos helped him out as he restructured. He swore he would not allow himself to be trapped like that again. Only, in a way, it had happened. Fiolax, a rubber company that manufactured automobile parts, was in a mess and while he had done nothing to put it there, Pelé was linked to the firm. Through previous poor legal advice, he had signed some documents that he never should have touched. While being only a 6 percent shareholder, Pelé had put himself into a bind as a moneybags figure who would rescue the company in case of difficulty. Fiolax was facing a government fine and had an outstanding loan that Pelé was on the book for, too. The combined total was $1 million.

When Pelé was a little boy in Bauru, the last thing his imagination could have conjured up was that he would be an adult with the wherewithal to pay out such an outrageous amount. Pelé could afford to handle the loan paybacks and the fine payment, though he was not happy about either development, and while he could swing the payment, it would take a considerable amount of financial juggling to pull it off.

Pelé could also envision his name being attached to an unsavory business not of his own making, but sure to embarrass him in the newspapers. The plan was to sell off some valuable assets and take a loss on a forced sale of property. How much would it cost to protect his good name? It was pretty expensive, Pelé figured out. Counting the elimination of the loan, the fine, and what he would lose from diminished profitability, Pelé's overall loss would be about $2 million.

The situation grieved Pelé. Somehow, he had allowed himself to be fooled into an untenable financial position for a second time and it was going to be costly to bail out. It was a blow to his pride, as well as his finances, the finances that he was using to support a family of four. The first time Pelé was trapped in a financial morass, he used his famous name for endorsements to gain money and his soccer skills as collateral with Santos. He managed to put that critical period of his life behind him and grew his finances once again from there.

Now, Pelé was in retirement, so he couldn't count on Santos' help for anything. He was no longer their marquee-level front man that could be used to fill the stadium seats anymore. It was either take big losses selling properties that he preferred to keep, ask for nationwide embarrassment and criticism by declaring bankruptcy for Fiolax, or dream up some type of completely fresh solution, none of which seemed readily available.

While Pelé liked to live well, it was within reason. He owned a Mercedes, but his other cars were two Volkswagens and an Opel. He moved his family into a $600,000 home which contained a movie theater that could seat 40. The main thing was that the large house was a secure compound. He and his immediate family needed the security. Dad was so famous that he could not go out to the store without being mobbed, or to a movie. Pelé was not going to be besieged for autographs in his own home. On some days, it would serve as a fancy prison. It was Pelé's policy to try never to refuse an autograph, and, so sometimes, he needed strategy when he left the house so as not to be trapped by a large group of people.

When he made his trips for Pepsi, goodwill trips, Pelé was putting himself into public scenes where he would sign many autographs. That was fine. Most of them were for kids, anyway. The Pepsi clinics unfolded this way: Professor Mazzei would speak about proper soccer techniques, and calling upon his background as a trainer he spoke about exercise habits and conditioning. Then, Pelé demonstrated the fundamentals of soccer techniques, from kicking and heading the ball to trapping the ball on the fly, as well as tackling and passing.

"My trips for Pepsi-Cola were really the most pleasurable travel that I ever made," Pelé said. "It put me in direct contact with children of all races and colors in all countries and in all languages. It constantly reminded me of a truth I had always known—there are no differences between children. On a football field, eager to learn and to practice their newfound knowledge, all children are alike in every sense. It is only when adults teach them hate or bigotry that they begin to change."[3]

Pepsi's plans were very ambitious. Before he knew it, Pelé's new life with the soft drink company had him traveling as much as he had with the national team and Santos. The travel was different, though. There was not as much pressure on Pelé to live up to being the great Pelé and score goals and lead his team to victory. The pressure to perform was minimal since Pelé could probably do the clinic in his sleep, while in mid-air, or standing on his head rather than hitting the ball with his head. The clinic road show included Pelé, Mazzei, an assigned company man, and a collection of soccer balls. Stops included Japan, Bombay,

Mauritius, Uganda, and Kenya. In Africa, Pelé saw tremendous gatherings of wild game, but was frightened when the pilot of his DC-3 had to circle the airfield once to scare herds of wildlife off the runway. The landing strip was dotted with potholes and that sight did not make Pelé feel much better.

The traveling clinic visited Nigeria and was packing up for a return to the United States when the plane was delayed leaving Lagos. The president of the country had been assassinated and a coup attempt was under way. The airport shut down overnight and a curfew was imposed. Foreigners were told to stay in their hotels. The existing government retained control and then imposed a period of mourning for the dead president, keeping the airport shut for nearly a week longer. Pelé's little group hooked up with a World Championship Tennis team that featured Arthur Ashe, Stan Smith, Bob Lutz, and Tom Ocker. They were in the same hotel, but when the trouble broke out, they slipped out to the American Embassy.

Both groups worked frantically to obtain seats on a plane that would leave the country and take them to the United States and agreed to help one another—whoever got reservations first would attach the other group. Pelé and the team were granted permission to head home after six days, though a brief stopover was made in Ghana on the way through Zurich to New York. While they had been delayed, others outside of Nigeria, reading reports of the violence, picked up a rumor that Pelé and his bunch had been imprisoned. Rosemeri believed them and was about to start lobbying for Pelé's release when he reappeared and made contact.

Although Pelé had followed through with his retirement from the Brazilian national team, and ultimately from Santos, too, consistently sticking to the plans he had announced, representatives from other clubs around the world, particularly in Europe, from time to time pitched him on making a return to the field for them. Their offers were substantial, significant amounts of money. Pelé was never tempted and he did not need the money when he retired. His business setback created a different set of circumstances for him, though, as 1974 turned to 1975.

There were few legitimate options, and none appealing to escape the Fiolax jam that Pelé thought over after his sobering discussion with

Xisto. He was going to make the bite-the-bullet deal that included selling off profitable properties to prop up Fiolax and clean the slate with that albatross of a company when a fresh idea popped into the discussion, a way for him to accomplish a few things at once.

One day, when Pelé was closing in on the master plan to settle the financial situation with a bit of pain, Xisto approached him to present an alternative—go to New York to play for the Cosmos. Two years had passed since Pelé had what he thought was his one-off meeting with Clive Toye, but as Toye had pledged, the Cosmos never lost interest in the player.

Pelé's first inclination was to reject the idea out of hand, but Xisto had done some homework. He consulted with Professor Mazzei and Mazzei accompanied him to this meeting, as did Pelé's brother who used the nickname Zoca, for a presentation that included Rosemeri as an intent listener as well. Pelé's friend came armed with a list of pros and cons on the Cosmos idea all sprinkled out on paper. While he professed to impartiality, Mazzei played the role of devil's advocate. Zoca was apparently the silent partner.

Mazzei went over the negatives first with an even-handed approach, and by the time he finished reading them aloud, Pelé was convinced Mazzei was against the idea. Among those items on the negative side of the lecture was the public perception of Pelé returning to active play when he had skipped the 1974 World Cup, retired from Santos, and told everyone that he had no intention of ever playing again. Although Pelé told everyone he would never play high-level soccer again, he was persuaded to change his mind Mazzei warned Pelé that being a black man in the United States was not the same as being black in Brazil—he might well face discrimination. Although he spoke English, he would have to improve his language skill. And it might well be that Kelly Cristina would be put back a year in school.

After what seemed like a long-winded argument against going to New York, Mazzei simply flipped over the piece of paper to present the points in favor of Pelé joining the Cosmos. He had 18 of those. The single biggest reason in favor of going was financial, Mazzei said. The Cosmos would likely pay him so much money that he would be able to pay off the Fiolax loan, pay the government fine, and still have money left over. The added bonus would be that he would not have to sell other holdings to cover those costs.

That alone was a big plus. There were others, though. The Cosmos were owned by Warner Communications, a huge company with a large footprint in many areas and one that had the power to make Pelé, now in retirement, even better known than he was. In addition, as Pelé had noted in the past as a simple observation, the United States was a backwater in soccer development compared to Europe and South America. But all of the ingredients were present for growth and expansion of the sport in that country and Pelé could be the catalyst.

Having Warner behind the team meant that a major corporation would guarantee his salary and that it would use its muscle to promote him in the one major country in the world where he was not as well-known. Another appealing aspect of playing soccer for the Cosmos was that the team's season ran about six months, not year-long like Santos, and would obligate him to play roughly from April to October at most. New York City also offered exceptional schools for Pelé's children, in particular, a United Nations school that would seem to be ideal.

When Mazzei finished his presentation, the first thing Pelé did was ask his wife how she viewed the matter. "It's your decision," Rosemeri said. "It's a lot of money to lose, this Fiolax matter, but if we have to lose it to keep your name clean we will. We won't starve without it. If you go to New York, the children and I will go with you happily."[4]

Perhaps if Rosemeri had adamantly opposed the idea of moving to New York, Pelé may have cut off discussion there, but she had tossed the soccer ball into his court. It was up to him. Pelé struggled with the concept of being forced to take a big financial loss to cover up a situation that he had not created. He would be losing money that he had intended for his children's security and that he had earned with hard work. Also, it was the second time something like this had happened to him where he had been shoved into a financial corner and he did not like the entire nature of it.

Pelé thought over all of the pros of making such a move and they were all legitimate. He also experienced a few moments of clarity about his own nature and truthfully admitted how much he missed playing soccer, participating before crowds of fans, doing the thing he was the best in the world at doing.

"It would also be nice to be back in uniform again," Pelé said, "feeling the wind of an open field on my face, the springy sod underfoot, matching my wits against a tricky opponent, feinting him out position, dribbling around him, passing off to a knowledgeable teammate who would know the exact moment to return the pass so I could feel the leather of my shoe strike the leather of the ball and see it curve past a startled goalkeeper into the net. I could almost feel the scream of Gooooaaaaallll in my throat again . . . while the crowds chanted 'Pelé! Pelé!'"[5] That daydream certainly did sound like a man who missed his calling.

Pelé instructed his advisors to get in touch with Clive Toye at the New York Cosmos' office to talk business.

Over the years Pelé had been offered significant sums of money to play for other top clubs around the world. The original approach from the Cosmos was nothing new in his world. Real Madrid, still one of the most famous soccer clubs on the planet, once tried to sign Pelé. So did Juventus. AC Milan was in there pitching, too. Pelé later said that some of the clubs were willing to go as high as $15 million to secure his talents.

In the 1970s, professional baseball, basketball, football, and hockey players did not sign multi-year, multimillion-dollar contracts. But Pelé did. His arrangement with the Cosmos—and the team's parent company Warner Communications—called for $4.5 million in payments directed his way. That was a fantastic sum of money for the time and in comparison to anyone else playing on a more popular American-based sports team, even if, as Pelé said, other soccer teams around the world would have gone higher. While the money would have been spectacular, the lifestyle would have been the same as the one he gave up with Santos. Constant travel, combined with constant matches all year long, with immense pressure on him to produce because he was not only Pelé, but because he was being paid a fortune.

The fortune was immense by sports standards, yet the Cosmos' situation was not as intense. In New York, Pelé would play half the year and also not have to worry about being as much under the microscope as he would if playing for another international powerhouse club.

Once Pelé gave his advisors the go-ahead to contact the eager Cosmos, and although both sides were willing, it still took six months to finalize a contract. Mazzei was the lead man on the negotiations and meetings were conducted in Rome, Belgium, Brazil, and the United States. Although tax experts, soccer experts, management experts, the player, the team, and attorneys were all deeply involved in finalizing the language of the plan, somehow the pending arrangement remained secret. Henry Kissinger, a big Pelé fan, and an acquaintance after meeting in the United States and at the World Cup, wrote a note in his role as Secretary of State constituting an invitation for Pelé to play in the United States.

Pele understood that having one of the most powerful men in the country on his side could help smooth his transition to American soccer. Right up to the last moment, Pelé was not sure he was doing the right thing, especially if the Cosmos expected him, approaching his mid-30s, to play as well as he had in his mid-20s.

One reason the deal was so complicated was because ancillary points were added. Pelé, who was already doing soccer clinics for children, not only in the United States, but around the world, wanted Brazilian children to benefit from his arrangement with the Americans, too. A clause was inserted saying that some American coaches would travel to Brazil and work with children to improve their skills in basketball, track and field, and swimming. This was a highly unusual insert in a personal sports contract and took some planning.

When it came to the dollars Pelé would be rewarded with for heading to the United States, the $4.5 million salary was ample. But in addition, Pelé would sign on for promotional work with the Licensing Corporation of America which, like the Cosmos, belonged to Warner Communications. Whatever endorsement deals were brought to the company because of Pelé, the proceeds would be split 50–50 between the player and the organization. Between salary and outside deals, Pelé stood to make more money through the Cosmos than he had made during his entire career with Santos.

From the first moment that Professor Mazzei presented the pro-and-con list to Pelé about joining the Cosmos, one of the foremost negatives—and one that concerned him—was what type of hit his reputation would take in Brazil. Millions of Brazilians had pleaded with Pelé not to retire. They had begged him to represent the country in the 1974 World Cup and he turned them down. He had bowed out of club play with his longtime affiliation Santos. He announced he was never going to play soccer for another club team. He was finished with the sport, on his way to assuming a new life.

And now, here he was, accepting riches to play for a team in another country, snubbing his countrymen in favor of foreigners. As Pelé expected, the immediate backlash was harsh. Critics called him a mercenary, just resuming play for the bucks. The Brazilian government, which had declared him a national treasure some years earlier, couldn't be happy about this. When he was younger and in his prime, the government passed that legislative declaration to ensure that he would never leave.

Efforts were made in the design of Pelé's contract to counteract governmental concern. That was one way the U.S. coaches provision helped—demonstrating that there would be benefits to Brazil if Pelé played in the United States. Warner Communications officials also sought the cooperation of the American government in this public relations endeavor and received an official statement indicating that the loan of Pelé from Brazil to the United States would produce warmer relations between the two countries. The maneuver proved successful with the Brazilian government even if there were some hardcore Brazilian soccer fans who probably never forgave him for this so-called betrayal.

Really, only a player of Pelé's stature would ever be in such demand near the end of his career in a team sport. His name was magic. His history was magnificent. He was probably the best known person in the world (with the possible exception at that time of Muhammad Ali), and most critically to Pelé's move, the time and circumstances in his career and U.S. soccer's standing in the world made the marriage an ideal one.

It was the right time in Pelé's life (his situation following retirement from Brazilian soccer and his business setback being paramount) and the right time in the life of U.S. soccer, with the one team in the country that could have managed such an earth-shaking maneuver being the one that saw the possibilities and had the patience to make a long shot into a reality.

Indeed, against very long odds, Pelé, the world's greatest soccer player, was about to become a New York Cosmo and play out his final days as a soccer hero in a country that knew his name better than it knew the rules of the game. For Pelé, it was a risk with a huge potential upside, but one well worth taking.

NOTES

1. Pelé and Robert L. Fish, *My Life and the Beautiful Game* (New York: Doubleday & Company, 1977), p. 262.

2. Ibid., p. 282.

3. Ibid., p. 296.

4. Ibid., p. 286.

5. Ibid., p. 287.

Chapter 12

NEW YORK, NEW YORK

Pelé publicly became a member of the New York Cosmos of the North American Soccer League on the afternoon of June 11, 1975, at the famous Manhattan 21 Club.

The man who needed no introduction to the soccer world was introduced to the American sporting public at a jam-packed event that was standing-room-only. As sportswriters who didn't know much about soccer fought for position to hear Pelé's words because they recognized that the arrival of the world's most famous athlete was news, the object of their curiosity seemed serene. He was dressed somewhat casually in a leisure suit, considered fashionable at the time, and wore a somewhat lighthearted accessory—a Big Apple pin attached to his clothing.

Contractual arrangements, after those six months of haggling, had been concluded the day before in the Bahamas. Pelé, who had made it everywhere else, was about to make it in New York. Rosemeri attended the press conference, but she stood in the background, taking in the frenzied scene. His children were not present, but daughter Kelly Cristina was eight years old at the time and son Edson, who had been nicknamed Edinho at a very young age, was four.

When questioned, Pelé spoke in his native tongue, Portuguese, through a translator, rather than risk making a faux pas in English. He understood the questions in English, but took care at this moment to make a good impression. Improvement in his English language skills, as suggested by his friend Julio Mazzei, would come gradually, but Pelé had already begun taking English lessons as the date for his arrival in the United States grew closer.

During his tours of the United States, Pelé recognized that the country had a lot of latent potential as a soccer-friendly nation, but had done little work to develop the game at the grassroots. He was not merely speaking from the standpoint of good public relations at this introductory meeting with the media—Pele had long felt this way. "Everyone in life has a mission," Pelé said, "and my dream is that one day the United States will know soccer like the rest of the world. This is the only country in which soccer was not a major sport and I had a dream that one day the sport would come here with my help. For the first time in Brazil's history we were exporting know-how to you, instead of importing it." [1]

Before the news conference adjourned, Pelé joked with the sports reporters, indicating there was one small snag with his Cosmos deal. "When I signed the contract they didn't tell me that I had to try out. But now the coach says I have to make the team." [2] Hah, hah, everyone laughed. The Cosmos had cleared roster space for Pelé obviously, but he did harbor a minor worry that his middle-aged soccer self might not be good enough to wow the American fans.

That much was true, but it turned out to be a pointless fear. Pelé was not the same player he was during his early days with Santos, but he was plenty good enough to make an impression. Almost immediately there was a simple, but powerful reminder that Pelé's name carried clout. When he first suited up for the Cosmos in about a week in an exhibition game against the Dallas Tornado at New York's Downing Stadium, television cameras were going to be on the scene to record the moment. Two companies, CBS in the United States, and Global TV, agreed to pay the Cosmos $50,000 for the television rights for Pelé's American debut. Compared to many other sports, the TV rights fee was minimal, but the game would otherwise never have been shown.

Without getting off his bum, at a press conference and just by joining the Cosmos, Pelé was already garnering much more attention for his team and the league in two ways than it would have on an otherwise quiet June day. In fact, closely following from afar, the *New York Times* had been on the case, a week earlier reporting that an agreement was imminent and the famous Pelé was about to grace their city.

In one of its early stories, the still-very-formal *Times* in those days featured Pelé as "Man in the News," but referred to him in a headline by his lengthy, full birth name. That changed in the body of the story, however, as the world's best newspaper tried to make sense of who the world's best soccer player was for its readership. "It is almost meaningless to call Pelé incomparable of peerless, or to use any other of the terms that glory an athlete's ability," the story began. "The name Pelé itself has become an adjective for the superlative."[3]

Before even signing his contract Pelé made a visible visit to Downing Stadium to watch the Cosmos play. He still was apparently playing it a bit coy at the time, though, because nothing had been inked. "If I return, it will be because of my love for soccer," he said. "I want to help soccer to grow in this country and I want to keep making publicity for Brazil."[4]

By this time in his life, Pelé had been interviewed thousands of times, but he seemed to understand that when he was asked questions that referred back to his earliest childhood and greatest achievements things that even the most casual of Brazilian soccer fan knew about him—that he was addressing a new audience. So, he told the *New York Times* how he had never wanted to be anything but a soccer player. He also spoke about the influence of his father.

Over the years, Pelé had told people about how his father was his role model and how important he was to his development, but he may not have said what he said this time terribly often. "I wanted to follow my father," Pelé said. "I thought he was the greatest soccer player who ever lived. He just never got a chance to prove it."[5]

The *Times* seemed to be on top of many of the details of Pelé's contract with the Cosmos ahead of the signing, if only the financial terms. Making the rounds was the suggestion Pelé was going to collect $7 million in salary, but Clive Toye, his Cosmos pursuer, denied that and revealed the true figure of $4.5 million. The Cosmos were already scheming as to how they would recoup the investment. During the 1975 season, the North American Soccer League was just 22 games long, but it was scheduled to increase to 30 the next season. It was anticipated that when Pelé made the rounds visiting the other teams in the league, more fans would attend, so the Cosmos made an arrangement with the league to obtain 50 percent of the gate from those teams. That would give New York the only such revenue-sharing plan in the league. It was designed to help the Cosmos get some payback for bringing the Brazilian superstar to the league. The team admitted that it hoped that Pelé's presence for a full season the next year might bring in $2 million more than it otherwise would have been able to earn.

It was interesting to note that the Cosmos, much like Santos, had plans to take advantage of Pelé being on the roster in other ways. Not that they commanded such large fees. Toye said that the Cosmos, as they were constituted without Pelé, could obtain some fees in Europe, but with Pelé, the payday would jump by 500 percent a game. "Now we can get $5,000 a game, plus expenses," Toye said. "With Pelé we should get $25,000 a game plus expense money."[6] Figuring on 12 exhibitions on a European tour, that would add $300,000 to the Cosmos' coffers.

As one of a small number of newspapers in the United States at the time which staffed foreign bureaus, the *New York Times* was also able to send a South American correspondent to rendezvous with Pelé in Brazil in advance of his trip north to sign the contract. It was clear from that interview, even before he reiterated the point at his news conference in New York City, that Pelé was going to stress his role as someone who would bring attention to U.S. soccer. He may have overdone it—certainly for the times—when he said that the game which the world calls football could be more popular in the United States than the game that Americans know as football.

"Soccer can be more popular than football in the United States because it's much more of a spectator sport," he said, "more technical, more ballet."[7] No one has ever gone broke relying on Americans' enjoyment of violence in their sporting events and few have ever made major profits comparing the favored games of the country to ballet.

While he did not use the word, Pelé saw himself as a savior of U.S. soccer, the one that could help put the sport on the map. Soccer was so ingrained in his life from an early age and was so ingrained in the

Although Pelé—seen here dribbling past opponent Alan Kelly while playing for the New York Cosmos—was the best player in the world, he always expressed great respect for the foes he came up against. (AP Photo)

culture of Brazil, he did not easily relate to a country which even among its sports fans could take it or leave it when it came to soccer. "What I find strange is that New York, which is the world capital of sports, ignores soccer, the most widely played sport in the world," Pelé said. "Football and baseball are so widely accepted there that people have forgotten soccer, but I am sure I can help revive it."[8]

That was partially what Pelé was going to be paid millions of dollars to do. He came from the perspective of a soccer-centric world, but had also seen the world. He had played in four World Cup tournaments and knew that in many countries daily activity virtually ceased if their national team was competing. By the mid-1970s, the estimated television audience for the World Cup was 900 million viewers. Pelé had been toasted and feted by kings and queens, presidents and prime ministers. He had been greeted by throngs of thousands at airports when he stepped off of an airplane. For years, he had been called "the king of soccer." He was the only player to score 1,000 goals and that number was a speck in his rearview mirror at that point with his total climbing over 1,200. Naturally cordial and a relatively humble man, Pelé was not someone who generally tooted his own horn. But he understood his place in the world soccer hierarchy, understood that he was the best soccer player who ever lived. When an American newspaper journeyed to Brazil to spend time talking to him, it would have been ridiculous to be too self-effacing. So, when asked for the scouting report on Pelé, why he was Pelé, he chose his words carefully.

"People say I have a little of everything," Pelé said, "but it's difficult to explain, the same as describing what Chopin has." Certainly, Pelé created great music in his own way. But when it came to detailing his best attributes, Pelé did not say that he could dribble the ball past anyone, or that he had a sixth sense that allowed him to control the ball and find small openings to score goals. He cited being "moral, (his) personality, perseverance, always the will to win" as the things that defined his greatness.[9]. Maybe that was just another way of saying that Pelé got where he was by being Pelé the person, and his skill was a gift from god. He actually used the phrase "God's divine gifts."[10]

Beyond reporting the scores of games, one thing sportswriters must do as a matter of course in their duties is to explain why an outstanding player is outstanding, what separates this athlete from his teammates, opponents, his contemporaries. Since Pelé stood just five feet, eight inches, and his weight was roughly in the 165-pound range, his physique was not especially imposing the way a highly muscled, huge football player was, or a very tall basketball player.

Even before Pelé charmed the press at the 21 Club, again the *New York Times* was unleashing a full-fledged report about Pelé's physical attributes. One thing everyone knew from watching him play was that he possessed incredible peripheral vision. He could see opposing defenders coming when it seemed as if the angle was impossible. Pelé was almost the embodiment of the old joke about mothers having eyes in the back of their head to spot wrongdoing by their children.

In Pelé's case, there had been medical tests illustrating what some of his special characteristics were that were so helpful to his success. "Pelé's heart when he is in training beats 56 to 58 beats a minute," the *Times'* analysis stated. "The heart of an average athlete in training beats 90 to 95 beats a minute. Pelé's aerobic capacity is such that he can repeat a great effort within 45 to 60 seconds. His peripheral vision is 30 percent greater than that of the average athlete."[11] *The average athlete.* Not the average person or the average man his age.

All of this was known because a few years earlier, Pelé had subjected his body to doctors' examinations at a laboratory, essentially to satisfy the curiosity of what made him tick. The final conclusion of the doctors was fairly straightforward: "Whatever this man might have decided to do in any physical or mental endeavor he would have been a genius."[12]

The rest of the New York newspaper world was trying to catch up to the *New York Times* by the time Pelé made his grand entrance to soccer in the United States and to the city that never sleeps. "You can say now in the world that soccer has finally arrived in the United States," Pelé said at the 21 Club. At the time, the Cosmos had 14 games left in the season and Pelé predicted he could score a goal a game as soon as he got used to the team style.[13]

Pelé was joining a team that by his standards competed in a minor league and wasn't even doing particularly well at that level of competition. The Cosmos were 3–6 on the occasion of the press conference and Pelé was going to miss one of those 14 remaining games. The Cosmos met the Philadelphia Atoms on the road and he was a spectator. The transition from employee of the team to the field was going to take a few days, but his integration into U.S. soccer was under way.

The player joined his new teammates on the field, but he was wearing street clothes. Pelé's mere presence, though, had an effect on the proceedings. Attendance topped 20,000 fans (who may have thought they were going to get Pelé in spikes), instead of Philadelphia's usual average of 10,000 people a game and those fans cheered him. As Pelé walked to the middle of the field, the fans yelled, "We want Pelé! We want Pelé!" They were going to get him, just not that night, at least not in soccer-playing form.

In baseball, one longstanding ritual is to have someone throw out the first pitch. It is a ceremonial gesture. On this night in Philadelphia, to announce his presence in the United States, Pelé was tossed a ball and he gave it a little kick. This was a symbolic move, a hint that there would be more to come.

With the simple action Pelé had inspired and teased the fans. It would have been a storybook end to the day if Pelé's presence had also inspired the Cosmos to victory, if he had provided a pep talk that led to a triumph. However, the Atoms won the game 1–0, in overtime. Well aware of his stature and how his words could sting because he was

Pelé, the Brazilian icon had made it a practice never to overtly criticize teammates that were less talented than he. Assuredly, over the years, there had been occasions where he had tiptoed around that approach to provide a player with the type of minor rebuke that hopefully would highlight a problem and fix it.

Although he knew what he was getting into—that was why he was on the scene, after all—that night, it seemed for those reading between the lines that Pelé, for the first time, truly recognized the gap in soccer play between the top echelon of the game in the United States and what he was used to seeing and engaging in. In other words, by Pelé's high, high standards, the Cosmos weren't very good. And they hadn't played especially well in that game, either. As soon as the game ended, Pelé was again surrounded by sportswriters who naturally enough wanted to know what he thought about how his new team had fared and what he thought of the caliber of soccer. It was not Pelé's role to insult. He was enough of a diplomat to know that he had to be cautious about what he said, though he didn't want to completely duck the truth, either.

"As was the case with the Vancouver game which I saw two weeks ago," Pelé said, "I found that the Cosmos have a number of good players, but their style is too individual. I thought the Cosmos' defenders played well, but their forwards were too slow. They were disorganized on the field and they didn't play well together as a team. I feel from what I have seen, here the game is more of a running game, where in Brazil it is more technical. But that doesn't mean you can't use the technique that you have." [14]

While Pelé used no such harsh words, what in essence he was saying was, "Boy, you guys have a long way to go to become any good. I'll do my best to help you, but it's going to be harder than I thought." There is no such written record of a declarative statement like that, but he almost assuredly said something similar to Julio Mazzei, or to Rosemeri around that time. He may have said it with a sigh to begin with, but that would have been a transitory emotion. His next move would be to roll up his sleeves and get down to the business of improving the Cosmos and selling American soccer to what previously had been either a skeptical or uncaring public.

At all times, Pelé tried to speak diplomatically about the quality of the players the Cosmos had. Sometimes, he was asked whether or not he was still a good player at age 34, and other times, he was asked how he would be able to play with players who were not nearly as talented. The questions zinged like a tennis ball back and forth to extremes.

"On every team there are great players, good players and just players," Pelé said. "I have seen the Cosmos. We have all classes of players. If, as I said before, the Cosmos hope that my coming to them will automatically result in a championship then they are mistaken. Every player on the team must work and be willing to work together to build a strong team."[15]

Pelé's American coming out party occurred on June 15, in the exhibition game against Dallas at Downing Stadium on Randall's Island. As had been announced, the contest was shown on American television and elsewhere in the world through a joint rights package—13 other countries watched the game. Also, about 300 media members, split about 50–50 between writers and photographers, representing 22 countries, requested credentials for coverage. Whatever Pelé did, especially on the pitch, was still big news. In a stadium built to hold about 20,000 or so fans for baseball, the Cosmos–Dallas game attracted 21,278 fans. The Cosmos had predicted attendance in the 18,000 range and that was double their previous high game.

At that point, Pelé had been officially retired from Santos for about nine months. While he said he had been working out, he had also spent a lot of time sitting at a desk. He was confident he would be fine on the field, but he was probably not in absolutely top condition. Julio Mazzei admitted as much on the eve of the game. Mazzei, who had been hired by the Cosmos to work part-time as a trainer, his original specialty with Santos, and as assistant coach with head coach Gordon Bradley of England, estimated that Pelé was at about 70 percent. "His timing is off a bit," Mazzei said. "Give him a few more days and he will be just fine."[16] Unsure of his condition, Pelé initially thought he might play just the first half.

Fans gave the stadium a festive feel by waving Brazilian and Santos banners and they held up signs reading "Thank You Brazil." One thing that added to the flavor of the game was Dallas' star, Kyle Rote Jr. Rote, who in 1973 was the North American Soccer League rookie of the year, and was also the son of former New York Giants American-style football star Kyle Rote. Rote Jr. was the type of homegrown player

American soccer was trying to build around and it was a bonus that he had a famous sports name.

After the game, Pelé praised Rote, saying, "To see an American-born boy with such good soccer skill is very pleasing. He really surprised me with some of the moves he made out there." [17]

The Cosmos started slowly and Dallas built a 2–0 lead at halftime. Pelé determined that he would continue to play the second 45 minutes and he engineered the New York comeback. The Cosmos cut the lead to 2–1 when Pelé set up teammate Mordecai Shpigler, an Israeli player previously acquired by New York. Pelé drew Dallas goalie Ken Cooper out of position and then fed Shpigler. Later, Shpigler set up Pelé. The ball was just outside the Dallas net in a crowd and Pelé out-jumped everyone to head the ball into the goal for the tying score.

That represented a rousing comeback, if not a victory, in the exhibition. The Cosmos put some fine play on display, yet at the same time it was obvious that Pelé and his teammates needed time to blend together. Numerous times passes were off the mark because they did not know where one another would be and they overall were not in synch. "We need a few more games together," Pelé said, "a chance to get to know each other before we can really start playing. But on today's performance I have no doubt we can become a very good team." [18]

It was a start.

To that point, Pelé had seen three other NASL teams. The Cosmos had lost 1–0 twice and tied 2–2, so he figured they would be as good as anyone. Alas, he hadn't seen the Cosmos play against the best teams, so making a mark over the last stretch of the season was going to be a bigger challenge than he expected. "Still, we were improving with age, even though our improvement could hardly be called spectacular," Pelé said. He did stress that he took great satisfaction in seeing the Cosmos' attendance mushroom when he and the team came to town or even at regular home games. That counted a lot for him. [19]

Where Pelé went, even as he and the Cosmos became used to each other well enough to complete the remaining games 7–6 together, pandemonium tended to follow. Soccer fans new to the game had been told he was a celebrity and they treated him as such. Soccer fans who knew the game—many of them U.S. immigrants—flooded teams with requests for tickets when Pelé came to town. Living in North America, this was something they never expected to see live and in person, only on television. Plus, they felt they had missed their chance altogether once Pelé retired. Sure, he was a bit older, but he was still the most important figure in the history of the game and to see him play in the flesh was irresistible.

Most of Pelé's Cosmos teammates were in awe of him at first, but they discovered that not only was he a very down-to-earth fellow, but he genuinely wanted to help them. He offered tips in practice and talked about teamwork and how they could all make one another better. Between the Dallas exhibition and the Pelé "opener" of sorts against Toronto, Tony Piciano, who was originally from Argentina, had played college soccer in the United States and now was a Cosmos player, explained what it was like to compete with Pelé on your side. "Sunday was my birthday," Piciano said. "During the first 10 minutes of our game against Dallas I was overawed and nervous. But being on the same field as Pelé was the greatest birthday present I could have received. Pelé relaxed me. He told me to take it easy and play my game, and I'm really grateful to him, as are all the players." [20]

Pelé's first appearance for the Cosmos in a league game was June 18 versus Toronto. Although Pelé did not score a goal, New York won the game 2–0, and more than 22,500 people filled Downing Stadium. More than that wished to attend, but couldn't get in. The team announced that more than 4,000 cars were turned away from the stadium parking lots.

Just how desperately soccer fans wanted to see Pelé, meet Pelé, touch Pelé, and revered Pelé was on display at a June 20 road game in Boston. This was one time the adulation spilled over. Like the scenes of hysterical girls pursuing the Beatles through the streets, Pelé was in danger of being loved to death. It wasn't enough for Boston fans to cheer him—mobs surrounded him and actually injured him.

The Boston Minutemen competed in a Boston University stadium designed to hold 15,000 fans. Sellouts were not a problem until Pelé came to town. About 20,000 people showed up, overflowing the seating and standing room areas. The fervor over Pelé's presence was heightened before the opening kick, and grew from there. About 79 minutes into the 90-minute game, the Cosmos took Pelé out of the lineup. He had scored a goal (later disallowed) that set off a frenzy in the fans. Not content to yell, scream, and applaud, fans invaded the field to get more personal with their congratulations.

In the scrum that followed, Pelé hurt his right knee and he twisted his side and sprained his ankle, all in the interests of self-preservation. A combination of efforts prevented additional injury to Pelé. He traveled with his own bodyguard, Pedro Garay. The Cosmos imported additional security. And Boston goalie Shep Messing helped shield Pelé from the worst of the gathering swarm. Boston won the game 2–1 as, intriguingly, the Minutemen suited up an old friend of Pelé's. Eusebio of Portugal was on loan and he scored a goal for Boston. "I never saw a soccer crowd go crazy like that before," Messing said. "I saw Pelé was hurt and I came out to help him. Some guy jumped me and I just pushed him off. Then the security men got there and helped him." [21]

Pelé even briefly disappeared from view under a host of fans, although Garay tried to shield him from more possible damage by throwing his body over his charge. Pelé left the field on a stretcher, which was a sobering sight, his uniform torn and his psyche a bit battered. It would not do at all to have the world's greatest soccer player dismembered by worshipping fans.

Toye, the Cosmos' general manager, demanded that the league be more on the ball in requiring extra security at stadiums on the road. Pelé admitted that the situation had unnerved him. "I was shaken up and scared," he said. [22]

Toye was infuriated. He had worked for years to gain Pelé's trust and bring him to the United States. Together, they shared a grand vision of raising the profile of soccer in the country and improving its quality. All of a sudden, he saw his grand scheme jeopardized by a group of rowdies. "I am concerned about his safety," Toye said after the Boston game. "Not because he is the greatest player, but because he is one of my players. I am concerned about the worst player in the world. I don't want anybody to get hurt. Unless I am personally assured he is going to be safe Pelé will not play in Rochester (the next location) or any other place in America. He is too precious a person to be treated like he was here. I am going to make sure of his safety, even if I have to get the United States Marines." [23]

There were no additional incidents approaching the Boston situation in magnitude or danger. Although one of the stereotypes of soccer around the world for Americans was that riots broke out all of the time, entire armies were needed to safeguard the players, and moats had to be built around fields. There were some truths inherent in the stereotypes because such crazed passions were let loose on occasion. What no one ever anticipated was a mini-soccer riot at a game in the United States.

No one doubted that passions were inflamed by Pelé's presence—it wasn't the Cosmos showing up that stoked the emotions. The New York franchise acted accordingly in terms of how to raise soccer awareness around the country and to get back some of its investment in Pelé. When the Cosmos were scheduled to play, they bought display ads in newspapers. While the reader could find the name "NY Cosmos" in the ad, the approach was built around the headliner. When the Boston Minutemen were scheduled to play at Downing Stadium, this was how the Cosmos promoted it: "PELÉ: THE GREAT ONE. Act Now! Don't Be Left Out of All The Exciting Pelé Action! 5-Game Pelé Ticket Package."

Presumably, the rest of the Cosmos were also going to show up so Pelé didn't have to play 1 against 11.

NOTES

1. Don Kowet, Pelé (New York: Atheneum, 1976), pp. 8–9.

2. Ibid., p. 9.

3. (No byline), "Soccer's Superlative: Edson Arantes do Nasci mento," The New York Times, June 4, 1975.

4. Ibid.

5. Ibid.

6. Gerald Eskenazi, "Prospects for Cosmos Take a Bullish Turn," The New York Times, June 5, 1975.

7. Marvine Howe, "Pelé Out to Sway U.S. Fans," The New York Times, June 5, 1975.

8. Ibid.

9. Ibid.

10. Alex Yannis, "Pelé: A Slim Figure of Athletic Perfection," The New York Times, June 10, 1975.

11. Ibid.

12. Ibid.

13. Paul Montgomery, "Pelé Signs with Cosmos: 'Soccer Has Arrived' Here," *The New York Times*, June 12, 1975.

14. Kowet, pp. 13–14.

15. Joe Marcus, *The World of Pelé* (New York: Mason/Charter, 1976), p. 153.

16. Alex Yannis, "World Awaits Pelé," *The New York Times*, June 15, 1975.

17. Marcus, p. 161.

18. Alex Yannis, "21,278 See Pelé Score and Cosmos Tie," *The New York Times*, June 16, 1975.

19. Pelé and Robert L. Fish, *My Life and the Beautiful Game* (New York: Doubleday & Company, 1977), p. 294.

20. Kowet, p. 43.

21. Marcus, p. 166.

22. Alex Yannis, "Cosmos Demand More Security for Pelé," *The New York Times*, June 22, 1975.

23. Ibid.

Chapter 13

COSMOS II, RETIREMENT II

Pelé liked New York. He was still a celebrity, but away from the soccer stadiums, he could almost function without being hassled by fans—depending on how much attention was drawn to him publicly as opposed to accidentally. His children were enrolled in the United Nations school, a highly sophisticated school that provided superior educational facilities and catered to the children of international diplomats stationed in the United States.

The Brazilian soccer player did not attend U.N. sessions, but his job was actually similar to the suit-wearing visitors from other countries. "I had come to get Americans interested in football and I saw it as my job to be as visible as possible," Pelé said. "I was taking to New York and New York was taking to me. Crowds were flocking to Cosmos games and soon it seemed that everyone knew who I was. Once I went to a baseball game with Dick Young, a well-known sportswriter who was skeptical about soccer taking off in the U.S. When people realized I was in the stadium there was pandemonium because everyone wanted to see me. I remember Dick Young saying—I was wrong. You really are famous." [1]

It was during Pelé's first season with the Cosmos that he uttered one of his trademark comments that is always associated with him. While 90 percent of the world refers to soccer as football, in the United States, it is always soccer and the sport of football is something clearly distinct. Pelé found it difficult to break the habit of calling soccer football when speaking with sportswriters and others even in casual conversation. He certainly knew the difference between the sports. But he took to highlighting the difference between the one game where feet rule the action completely and the other, where there is much more physical play and contact and protective gear is needed by calling soccer "a beautiful game."

The description changed slightly to "the beautiful game" and Pelé not only used it with some regularity, others began to use the wording, either in attribution to his original statement, or on their own. "It must have resonated," Pelé said, "since the 'beautiful game' is probably my most commonly repeated phrase."[2]

On the field, the Cosmos became an attraction. In the pre-Pelé portion of the season, the Cosmos might attract 10,000 fans. After Pelé came aboard, soccer fans—old ones and converts—flocked to Downing Stadium for home games, doubling attendance, and opposing teams drew their largest crowds of the year when New York came to town.

TV and newspaper coverage of the Cosmos increased significantly. Before Pelé joined, the club stories were done irregularly. After Pelé joined the club, newspapers even traveled to away games to report on the contests, though the main reason they spent the money was to keep track of Pelé doings. It was possible another mini-riot would break out like the one in Boston and that would be newsworthy. Pelé might drop a bombshell of a statement and that could newsworthy. Or, he could simply play as Pelé could and that would be newsworthy.

On a late June trip to Rochester, New York, the Cosmos defeated the Lancers 3–0 before more than 14,000 spectators. The Lancers had been averaging about 4,000 fans a game.

Those in charge of security, conscious of the Boston incident and the Cosmos' clamor for more protection, came through. There were dozens of additional security personnel on alert for a peaceful evening. Pelé played very well, finding open teammates with impressive passes, and scoring a goal.

Just two days later, the Cosmos and Pelé treated a new audience to a command performance in Washington, D.C. Not only did the game draw more than 35,000 fans, Pelé scored two goals, set up two more with assists, and the Cosmos won 9–2.

The biggest problem for the Cosmos, who were definitely an up-and-down team, was whenever Pelé couldn't play. He suffered a thigh injury in a game and missed two games. Attendance dropped and the Cosmos, at their best a slightly above .500 team slipped slightly below .500.

While Pelé frequently shone on the field, sometimes using his finest, polished moves to get open, he earned clear shots at the net, but missed. It turned out that the ball used for NASL play was different than the ball used in international games and it was something Pelé had to get used to and adjust to when he kicked. "The ball here is softer and lighter than it is in Brazil and if you hit it as hard as you do in Brazil, it's going to go off on an angle and take off over the bar," Pelé said. "It will take me some time to get my kicks adjusted to the ball."[3]

One of the first things Pelé did after checking out the Cosmos on the field was to suggest to management that it bring in a couple of other players to help out. Pelé actually participated in the raiding of the Santos roster—or at least the borrowing of a couple of players. Nelsi Morais, another Brazilian, and Ramon Mifflin, who was from Peru, kept Pelé company with the Cosmos and four additional South American players were added to the team. The blend did not work as well as everyone thought it might and even Pelé admitted that not everyone brought in was worthy of the competition. That was somewhat of a revelation—that maybe the North American Soccer League brand of play was better than many believed. In any case, having too many imports was counter to the long-term goal of growing American soccer. There were enough top Europeans and South Americans playing that to be competitive a team did have to recruit outside the nation's borders, but it was imperative that in the long run Americans be nurtured and groomed to play in the best leagues in the world.

"The South American experiment failed, no doubt about it," said Cosmos coach Gordon Bradley.[4] That assessment did not include Pelé, who was now the face of the franchise and the face of the sport in the United States. Never much of a night owl, Pelé was expected to mingle more with the trendy people at Warner Communications events, so he met Frank Sinatra, Mick Jagger, Woody Allen, Michael Jackson, and many more well-known personalities. Once, heading into the Warner office, Pelé's presence touched off a clamor for his autograph among those recognizing him. He scribbled his name several times on the run and ducked into an elevator with another man, only to find out it was actor Robert Redford who was bemused at being ignored. "No one paid any attention to me!" Redford said while laughing. [5]

Pelé appeared on *The Tonight Show with Johnny Carson*, and instructed the comedian as he booted a ball around with him on the stage. Carson wore sneakers. That appearance took place in conjunction with a trip to Los Angeles for a game.

Pelé visited with President Gerald Ford, who had once starred in that other type of football as a collegian at the University of Michigan, on a trip to D.C. to play the Diplomats. Although he was in reality quite athletic, Ford had stumbled in public in few times and had been made out to be quite clumsy. Still, he kicked a soccer ball around with Pelé, too, outdoors, not indoors like Carson.

The meeting with Ford was quasi-official—it added heft to the U.S.–Brazil connection that was a byproduct of Pelé's contract. Ford officially welcomed Pelé to the country in a ceremony in the White House Rose Garden. Then, he said to Pelé, "Show me how you do it." Pelé bounced a ball off his foot repeatedly and without interruption. Not terribly surprisingly, the president did not match Pelé's style. Pelé did leave Ford with a Cosmos pennant as a souvenir.

Another time, Pelé, who had his picture painted by Andy Warhol, bumped into movie director Steven Spielberg who joked, "I am going to film you playing football on the moon because that's the only place you haven't played football yet." [6]

One of Pelé's favorite hobbies was fishing and he tried to fish when he could squeeze out free time on his road trips. Sometimes, it worked out. Sometimes, he didn't have enough time to make a side trip to a lake or river he wanted to visit. Once, on a trip to Seattle, Pelé had the itch to fish, but couldn't go anywhere. No problem. The suite he was sharing with Julio Mazzei overlooked the harbor. The two men decided to fish from their window, dropping lines into the water for the exercise with little hope of catching anything. They were surprised. Responding

As an indicator of his popularity, Pelé was invited to demonstrate some of his soccer ball-handling magic on The Tonight Show with Johnny Carson *in 1973.* (AP Photo)

to their yells, Pelé's bodyguard Pedro tore into the room where he saw Pelé and Mazzei attempting to subdue a couple-foot-long baby sand shark.

The North American Soccer League season concluded with mixed results for the Cosmos. The team did not win as many games as was hoped and was eliminated early in the playoffs. However, the brilliance of wooing Pelé paid off 1,000-fold in terms of publicity, produced additional streams of revenue, and made the Cosmos a much bigger brand name.

After the season ended, Pelé joined the Cosmos for an overseas exhibition tour that took them to Sweden, Turkey, Norway, Italy, and Haiti. People now knew the Cosmos overseas because Pelé was affiliated with them. In a matter of months, Pelé had helped raise the profile of his team and American soccer in the United States and abroad. It was an eventful, worthwhile, and fascinating season.

He scored just 15 goals in 23 appearances, but it was only a beginning. The year 1975 was in the history books and it was an historic one for American soccer. The door had been cracked open to worldwide acceptance and Americans for the first time showed signs of becoming bigger fans of the game. Pelé had led them there and after a few months' rest, he would resume the quest for a more successful on-field record for the Cosmos in 1976.

Actually, what passes for rest in Pelé's world was simply not competing. He was always traveling, taking care of business, and after the one-year trial session with Pepsi-Cola, he had re-upped long term. He loved running clinics for kids in small towns or big cities, in places where he spoke the language, or in places where someone had to translate. Recalling that Pelé signed on with Pepsi when he was retired, his value was only enhanced when he signed with the Cosmos and began playing in the United States.

The Pepsi trips provided Pelé with entrée to spending time with children and he tried to put light into their eyes by transmitting the joy of soccer to them. "It put me in direct contact with children of all races and colors in all countries and in all languages." [7]

Pelé and his family reunited with the relatives in Brazil over Christmas and then returned to New York, where his children's classes resumed. While Pelé's English had improved, his wife and kids spoke fluently. Their full-time residence for these Cosmos years was in New York, not Brazil, living in a Manhattan apartment.

The first round of excitement about Pelé's arrival in the United States had worn off and the Cosmos wanted to build a fresh, winning team with new faces. The roster was going to be drastically different, but that wasn't the only change. Gordon Bradley had moved to vice-president of personnel and a new coach, Ken Furphy, took over for the 1976 season.

Another Englishman, Furphy had played for years and had coached for a decade and a half.

Pelé felt Furphy's credentials were in order, but soon took issue with his style. Pelé felt the new coach was too rigid and his emphasis on defense versus the attacking style Pelé thrived in made for incomplete soccer in the star's mind. Pelé also disagreed with use of some of the personnel. He felt some of the best players were wasting away on the bench. Then, the Cosmos made a huge move, in soccer circles so big it was like bringing a second Pelé to the team. New York signed Giorgio Chinaglia, the Italian superstar, who was also a friend of Pelé's. That gave the Cosmos a phenomenal one-two scoring punch.

While Pelé was the name that gave the Cosmos and the league credibility the year before, Chinaglia was a brilliant acquisition as well. Not only was Chinaglia also world-famous, but he was seven years younger than Pelé and still in his prime. It was really the addition of Chinaglia that helped make the Cosmos a winner. An explosive, deadly scorer, Chinaglia was the NASL's leading scorer his first year, in 1976, and he ultimately scored more than 400 goals for the Cosmos, including appearances in a small number of indoor games.

The first game Pelé and Chinaglia played together, they each scored two goals and the Cosmos won 6–0. Yet, New York did not mesh smoothly. Pelé and Chinaglia were individually brilliant, but the offense did not maximize the use of other players and when those two couldn't manufacture goals on their own and wanted to pass to set someone up, frequently no one was there. The potential for greatness was there, so it was frustrating. Eventually, Furphy left his coaching job and Bradley dropped down from the front office again to take over the reins.

In the last game of the season, New York crushed Miami, 8–2. Chinaglia scored five goals and Pelé added two more. New York finished second in the standings with a 16–8 record. The Cosmos made the playoffs, but lost one game shy of the finals. They were well-positioned for the 1977 season with a powerful lineup and one that had jelled.

Pelé's scoring had brought him to a career total of 1,250 goals (his final total would be 1,283). This called for a return visit to the 21 Club for a different type of event. The Pony Sporting Goods Company decided that the performance was worthy of a special award, so it created a 24-carat, gold-encrusted soccer shoe as a gift for Pelé. He wasn't going to kick anything with that shoe, which certainly was symbol of how far he had come in the game. When he was a child in Bauru, he couldn't even afford soccer shoes. Now, he had one that was too valuable to wear.

When Pelé agreed to join the Cosmos, he signed a two-year contract. That contract expired at the end of the 1976 season. There was more evidence in his mind that his body was aging and that he could not play at the same pace as he had when younger. Still, the Cosmos season was so much shorter than the Santos season, there was really no comparison and even with the addition of some exhibition tours, the strain on his body did not come close to matching what he endured when he was playing in Brazil. So, he signed a one-year extension to return to the Cosmos for the 1977 season. "I didn't know whether 1977 would prove to be my final season as a player," he said. "I just wanted to do the best for the club and was excited by the further changes that were taking place, all of them it seemed, underlining the Cosmos' position as a force to be reckoned with in American soccer."[8]

The fact that Pelé was still playing the game, even if it was in New York, and even if it was supposedly against inferior competition, remained on the minds of Brazilian fans. As another World Cup approached in 1978, he began hearing more and more about the idea of him rejoining the national team for a fifth World Cup appearance. He did not dismiss the suggestions out of hand, although he would be 38 at the time, only half-heartedly saying he would think about it. That alone was a major concession. Other players of that age or older had represented their countries in World Cup play, so it would not be unprecedented. The notion was far-fetched, but wasn't instantly ruled out. One thing the great Pelé would not have wanted to be, though, was a mere figurehead, invited along for the ride because of the grandiosity of his past more than what he might contribute to the present. That would not appeal to him at all and it might not be something that his supporters were thinking about. Truth be told, however, Brazilian Pelé fans just wanted to see him in back in uniform wearing the home country colors, whatever his role.

There was no doubt, though, that Pelé made the right decision in choosing to play for the Cosmos in 1977. With the players, coaches, administration, all of the important pieces coming together, New York was in for a phenomenal year. Pelé and Chinaglia were ably supported by other players and their games became events. Only two years earlier, it was a pretty big deal when the Cosmos filled Downing Stadium with about 23,000 fans.

When it came time for the 1977 playoffs, the Cosmos played at the Giants Stadium at the Meadowlands in New Jersey and attracted 78,000 fans to see them whip the Fort Lauderdale Strikers 8–3. The Cosmos advanced to the championship game in Portland, Oregon, for the North American Soccer League title and bested the Seattle Sounders. Chinaglia scored the winning goal in a 2–1 contest.

The Cosmos were committed to a post-season world tour that took the New York club to Japan, Venezuela, Trinidad and Tobago, China, and India, Pelé's last stand, so to speak, before returning to Giants Stadium for one more rousing special game on October 1.

"The end was in sight now," he said. There would be no one more World Cup. Pelé knew it was time to retire on the cusp of his 37th birthday. "On my return I knew I would have to face the emotional turmoil of my very last game."[9]

Pelé had already been through a last game, and was surprised to even have this three-year extension to his career. But this time, when he pulled on the uniform, he knew it really was the last time as a pro. This was a specially arranged game between the Cosmos and Santos. In the first half, Pelé wore the Cosmos uniform and scored a goal. In the second half, he wore Santos' colors, but couldn't score. The Cosmos won the game 2–1. A shirtless Pelé was carried around the stadium, waving a small Brazilian flag in one hand and a small American flag in the other. "Again, the tears flowed down my face as I received the cheers of the crowd, but this time, as the rain came down, I didn't bother wiping them away," Pelé said.[10]

That time, on that date, October 1, 1977, Pelé retired as an active soccer player—for good.

NOTES

1. Pelé, *My Life in Pictures* (New York: Simon & Schuster, 2008), p. 74.

2. Ibid.

3. Joe Marcus, *The World of Pelé* (New York: Mason/Charter, 1976), p. 163.

4. Alex Yannis, "Cosmos: Experiment That Failed," *The New York Times*, August. 5, 1975.

5. Pelé, p. 74.

6. Ibid.

7. Pelé and Robert L. Fish, *My Life and the Beautiful Game* (New York: Doubleday & Company, 1977), p. 296.

8. Pelé, p. 75.

9. Ibid.

10. Ibid., p. 76.

Chapter 14

THE REST OF THE STORY

Pelé's father, Dondinho, and Waldemar de Brito, the two biggest influences in his early soccer life, were present at Giants Stadium for his last game. They had traveled thousands of miles to view the end of the career they had jump-started what seemed to be thousands of years earlier.

The last match of Pelé's career, bringing together Santos and the Cosmos, was covered by 650 sportswriters and was broadcast on television to 38 countries. A massive party followed the exhibition match, with the players, friends, comrades over the years, and many others invited. Some of the greatest soccer players in history attended besides, of course, Pelé. Carlos Alberto from Brazil was in the house. So was Bobby Moore from England and Franz Beckenbauer from West Germany.

Also present was heavyweight boxing champion Muhammad Ali, the only other man on the planet perhaps as universally known at that moment as Pelé and who was known for his proclamation, "I am the greatest!" Ali hugged the soccer player and announced, "Now there are two of the greatest!"[1]

The year 1977 marked the end of Pelé's competitive soccer seasons but he wasn't sure precisely what he wanted to do next with his life.

Pelé holds the spoils of victory, surrounded by teammates. For most of his playing days, when he was not representing the Brazilian national team, Pelé competed for a club named Santos. With Pelé as the driving force, Santos regularly won major competitions. (AP Photo/Nelson Antoine)

Almost simultaneously, a remarkable thing happened that essentially codified in an unusual manner what Pelé had done and become over the decades. On September 27, 1977, the United Nations gave Pelé a certificate declaring him to be "A Citizen of the World."

Soon after retirement, Pelé became a goodwill ambassador for FIFA, the governing body of soccer worldwide, and then he went to work for UNICEF, the United Nation's Children's Fund which is the agency that aids children suffering from hunger or disease.

In 1978, Pelé and Rosemeri became parents for a third time with a second daughter, named Jennifer. However, Rosemeri informed Pelé that she was weary of his worldwide travels and wanted a divorce. Pelé really never had slowed down. The couple separated after 12 years of marriage and their divorce was finalized in the Dominican Republic in 1982.

Although retired from soccer, Pelé renewed his commitment to do promotional work for Warner Communications with a fresh, 10-year contract and maintained his home in New York City. He admitted that at that point in his life as a single man, "there were distractions," which he admitted meant going out with many women and attending parties. One of his pals at the time was the former British soccer star George Best, who during his career was compared to American football star Joe Namath in terms of his celebrity, playboy lifestyle. In fact, Best was so talented and famous that at one time the Cosmos sought to hire him before they solidified their deal with Pelé.

Pelé said he dated models and beauty queens during this part of his life, but did not wish to get married again. That changed much later, after what began as a friendship with a Brazilian-born singer named Assiria Seixas Lemos, who was then married. Many years passed before Assiria got a divorce, became single again, got serious with Pelé, and then they married in 1994. About two years later, the couple had twins, Joshua and Celeste, named for Pelé's mother.

Eventually, Pelé and his second family moved back to Brazil, and he served the government as minister of sport between 1995 and 1998, though Pelé and Assiria divorced in 2008.

When Pelé retired, his goals total was 1,283. However, over the following years, he periodically appeared in games for charities and kept on scoring. Those goals are not counted in his official lifetime total, but he did score almost 100 additional times, concluding with 1,375 goals.

One of the key reasons why Pelé ended his first retirement in order to play for the New York Cosmos was to popularize soccer in the United States. His name was like magic and his personality was magnetic and wherever he traveled in the United States, crowds turned out to see him, talk with him, meet him, and especially to watch him play. In the short term, Pelé's three years with New York were very successful. He helped build his team into a champion, and in what was astonishing for the time, played before 78,000 people in a New York stadium.

In the long run, Pelé was correct that the United States was a sleeping giant in soccer and that someday sports fans would grow to love the game and appreciate its nuances. However, that took a lot longer to happen than Pelé envisioned and it was a bumpy ride.

Perhaps a foundation was laid by the North American Soccer League and by Pelé's contributions, but for many years, those foundations were just that. It took millions upon millions of dollars, energetic figures with vision and determination, and the winning over of youth to the game—and time spent for them to grow up—before soccer moved up in the hierarchy of American sport.

The original North American Soccer League that Pelé competed in was founded in 1968, but was out of business by 1985. It took a number of years to recover, although future American soccer players were influenced by watching Pelé and other stars of the era such as Georgio Chinaglia when they were kids.

In 1994, the United States hosted the World Cup. At the time, it was considered to be a huge leap of faith to turn over the FIFA showcase to a country that was not only second tier in the sport, but which had no professional league operating at the time. Yet, the U.S. World Cup was a smash hit, with tremendous attendance, and, in 1996, Major League Soccer was born as a successor to the original North American Soccer League. Since then, the caliber of play in the United States and American successes in major international events for both men and women have built the audience for soccer. Pelé lived to see the elevation of soccer into the top group of American sports leagues. In 2009, a league called the North American Soccer League was introduced again, but it is a minor league compared to the Major League Soccer level of play. However, in 2010, that new league introduced a franchise called the New York Cosmos—and Pelé was named honorary president of the team.

Taking on teams with long histories of success, the American men have improved gradually over the last two decades. However, the American women have been a world power since winning the first women's World Cup in 1991. The Americans started on a more level playing field because soccer for women was new to many countries. The United States has mostly held a stranglehold on the biggest prizes, also winning the 1999 World Cup and four Olympic gold medals.

More than 90,000 people watched the United States beat China 5–4, in the 1999 World Cup final, the largest crowd ever to attend a women's sporting event. The U.S. team, which was founded in 1985, has ranked No. 1 in the world regularly throughout the 2000s.

As a prolific, even voracious, goal-scorer, Pelé the center-forward, wore the No. 10 jersey that defines the position. Over the decades, Pelé was probably asked a thousand times what made him great. The related implication of the question was also what made a center-forward great. A few years ago, Pelé, who tries to remain relatively restrained when asked if he is the greatest, made a list of who, in his mind, are the best players who have ever worn No. 10 for their clubs and countries.

At the time, he summed up the attributes of the man who plays the central scoring role.

"He is a goal scorer, a creator, a target man, a team player, but also someone who has to be ruthless and selfish—greedy, even—to fulfill his task," Pelé said. "The cost of failure can be merciless, in the form of humiliation and outright hate. The potential rewards are both glorious and glamorous. No wonder we are a breed apart."[2]

In the decades since Pelé retired, there has been little competition from even the most ardent supporter of another superstar, suggesting that he was better than Pelé. The only other player to gain any measure of significant traction in the argument was Diego Maradona of Argentina. Maradona, in his early fifties, is now a coach. He led Argentina to the 1986 World Cup championship, commanded millions of dollars in salary, but has been embroiled in controversy because of drug problems, sitting through a 15-month FIFA suspicion for cocaine use.

Pelé did not rank his "10s" in order, but he did examine Maradona's credentials. "Diego Maradona was an unbelievable No. 10," Pelé said, "in many people's eyes the best footballer the world has ever seen. Certainly, few players have dominated a tournament like the Golden Boy did in 1986. He inspired his teammates to victory, almost winning matches on his own with his skill, pace and mesmerizing control."[3]

Among the other greats at that position Pelé singled out for praise were: Eusebio, his rival at the time of his own playing career; German Gerd Muller; Brazil's Garrincha; France's Thierry Henry, now playing in the United States; and Dutch sensation Johan Cruyff.

By dissecting the attributes of those players, their skills and abilities, their will to win and their leadership qualities, Pelé was attempting to do what so many reporters had asked of him since 1958—explain what made him tick. Pelé had not always been successful in translating his self-scouting report in understandable terms. The task was always made more difficult by the fact that Pelé did not wish to seem boastful. Another type of star, a Joe Namath or George Best, who were known for their kidding around, making predictions, and living colorfully, might have simply blurted out that they were the best and that's the way it was. But Pelé was never going to do that, was never going to brag in such a manner.

It had to be left for others to describe him, his gifts, his talents, his ability to do things with a soccer ball that most other players would never think of attempting, never mind pull them off successfully. The fact was that Pelé was unstoppable at times, so blessed with speed, that much-talked about peripheral vision, and the instinct to either create openings or seize the advantage based on the narrowest gap of space he spotted.

If Pelé wouldn't, or couldn't, do it, it was left for others to proclaim his greatness on the soccer pitch. Teammates or opponents, the men who shared the field with him were the closest to the man, sometimes even banging into him as he out-dueled them for the ball, out-jumped them for control of a pass, swerved around them if he darted one way. They were the beneficiaries of his maneuvers, or victims of them. They saw him in a way no other people could, not the fans in the stands, or those at home watching on television.

Following a game against the Vancouver Whitecaps, defender Lee Wilson said his teammates told him that he would be OK that day because Pelé wouldn't try too hard since it was only an exhibition. "After the game I told them that any time they want the assignment of guarding him, they're welcome to it," Wilson said. "I was faked out many, many times. I've never seen a man read the game so well in my life."[4]

One of the Cosmos' North American Soccer League opponents was the Washington Diplomats and when the teams met, invariably, Roy Wilner was assigned to cover Pelé. That was just asking for trouble each game, he discovered. He finished the encounters feeling he had been run through a blender. In the most obvious compliment a player can offer to an opponent, Wilner asked Pelé for his autograph. "I've never asked an athlete for his autograph before in my life," Wilner said. "But after what he put me through, I just had to get his name on the game program. He's not only the greatest soccer player in the world, he's one of the finest men I've met."[5]

Even George Best, who is regarded as perhaps the greatest British soccer player in history and was a contemporary of Pelé's, gives him credit. Best said he was not frustrated by coming in second in best-player polls all of the time during the arc of their careers.

"The reason Pelé is the greatest of all time is because he played for Brazil," Best said. "I played for Northern Island. Therefore it is a compliment to be mentioned in the same breath as someone who played for a nation that has now won the World Cup four times. (It is up to five.) The team I played for at the international level never won anything."[6]

The insertion of Pelé into a set-in-its-ways culture of the United States besotted with baseball, football, basketball, and hockey called for more than his superlative skill set to make an impact. He had to be smooth, charismatic, and charming, as well. Pelé in public had to be able to woo a population uneducated in soccer to a soccer stadium to make them understand it was a "beautiful game."

If no one had gone to watch Pelé, no matter what he did on the field, including making bicycle kicks often enough to complete the Tour de France, blind, cross-field passes, dribbling around other players as if he was Oscar Robertson, none of it would have mattered. If he performed in the anonymity of the empty stadium, nothing would have been accomplished.

To make his case, Pelé had to state it first with his personality, and then convince people with his showing. He was able to do that.

"He is Babe Ruth and the Rolling Stones, Billy Graham in one dramatic box-office package," wrote New York Post sports columnist Larry Merchant in 1975 before Merchant became better known as a boxing television commentator. "He could sell out Siberia. Reason being that he speaks an international language, drawn into the marrow from the cradle, and soccer is the most popular game on earth."[7]

Over a period of a few decades, being the greatest star in the most popular game on earth transformed Pelé's life. He was born into poverty in a small community in Brazil, so poor he played for a team distinguished by its inability to afford shoes. In a short time, he became the best and most famous soccer player in the world, leading his county to championships on the world stage. Eventually, he attained great riches and because he spoke that international language with his feet as much as his vocabulary, Pelé morphed into the most recognizable face on the planet earth. He was televised to nearly a billion people at once, yet was also known to people who had never watched a television set.

In 2005, in what was seen as a bold move, Pelé became a spokesman for the male virility enhancement drug Viagra.

As he approached his 70th birthday, Pelé was reflective about all he had experienced and all he had seen. "I have achieved more than I could ever have imagined," he said. "I've had everything a man could hope for. It has been a thrilling life. The joys have outnumbered the sorrows, many times over."[8]

Yet, as he passed his 72nd birthday, Pelé was deeply engrossed in new efforts that were bound to provide him with great excitement over the coming years. His home country was on the verge of being identified with the world's biggest sporting events not once, but twice in the immediate future.

Brazil was designated as host for the 2014 World Cup and as the host for the 2016 Summer Olympics. It was a dual honor that would place the nation in the world's spotlight for a period of years. As Brazil's greatest athlete, and already viewed as a goodwill ambassador, Pelé, in a sense, would play the role of individual host, welcoming the youth of the world to Brazil for sports and games.

For so many years, Pelé had globe-trotted around the world covering so many miles, he could have subsidized his own airline. Now in his old age, the world was coming to him, and not just the soccer world where he reigned supreme, but the entire sports world.

A hint of how well-remembered and how well-regarded Pelé remained in the world's eyes was offered in London at the end of the 2012 Summer Olympic Games when Pelé appeared. Near the end of the Games, Pelé was awarded an honorary doctorate from the University of Edinburgh—a notable achievement for someone who as a youngster initially was a fourth-grade dropout before returning to his schooling. "To be a great player is a gift from God, but to be a great man means always to respect people," Pelé said at the event. "I want to bring people together all over the world. We are all the same. We are all the son of God. I am the brother of everyone around the world."[9]

On the last day of the Games, Pelé made a public appearance in London at a sporting goods store in the famed Carnaby Street shopping area and it was as if he had never left the sport. He had a scheduled one-hour autograph signing at Soccer Scene, but more than 1,000 people mobbed the store and the street in front of it to either meet Pelé or catch a glimpse of him. There were far too many people on hand for Pelé to sign for them all and police sought to clear out the neighborhood even as Pelé waved to his fans.

When his time was up, Pelé could not linger because he was scheduled to appear on the field for the soccer final 30 minutes later. He was hustled out the back of the store, but one young man who realized that was the plan caught Pelé's attention by yelling to him in Portuguese. Pelé stopped and provided an autographed picture, rewarding the young man's effort and ingenuity. It was almost like his playing days when Pelé set up teammates for a goal.

Pelé was also in London as a spectator for the men's Olympic soccer final. He is the only man to play for three World Cup champions, but Brazil had never won the gold medal in the Games. Pelé hoped to witness such a victory, but his countrymen fell to Mexico and had to settle for the silver medal. The Brazilians probably could have used an assist from Pelé that day.

On the final night of the London Games, when the traditional Olympic handover takes place, ending the current Games and beginning the lead-up to the next Games, which are scheduled for Rio de Janeiro, all as part of the closing ceremony, Pelé was an unexpected participant.

His surprise appearance, arms outstretched, before the Brazilian national anthem was played, caught the 80,000 spectators in the stadium off-guard, but when he was recognized, the fans roared in delight. After the Games ended, Pelé raved about the hospitality, and the smooth-running London operation, and the host country's friendliness. He said it should serve as a role model for Brazil for the upcoming World Cup, as well as the Olympics.

"They have definitely set an example of what you need to do," Pelé said.

One of the things Brazil needs to do is to keep its greatest athletic hero front and center during the 2014 World Cup and the 2016 Olympics. The man who still does not know how he acquired the name Pelé has made it the most famous name in the world through magnificence on the soccer pitch, as well as through his grace off the field.

If given the opportunity—and the miracle of time availability—no doubt Pelé would shake the hand of every single one of the hundreds of thousands of people destined to visit Brazil to watch the beautiful game and what the world hopes will be beautiful Games.

NOTES

1. Pelé, *My Life in Pictures* (New York: Simon & Schuster, 2008), p. 76.

2. Pelé, *10: What Makes a Great Player from the Master* (Newbury Park, CA: Haynes Publishing, 2010), p. 110.

3. Ibid.

4. Don Kowet, *Pelé* (New York: Atheneum, 1976), p. 110.

5. Ibid., p. 85.

6. Harry Harris, *Pelé: His Life and Times* (New York: Welcome Rain Publishers, 2001), p. 150.

7. François Thebaud, *Pelé* (New York: Harper & Row Publishers, 1976), p. 131.

8. Pelé, *Life in Pictures*, p. 84.

9. Henry Winter, "Pelé in Britain to Help Brazil's Push for Elusive Gold against Mexico at Wembley," *London Telegraph*, August 9, 2012.

APPENDICES

Appendix 1.   Pelé Quick Facts

Name	Edison Arantes do Nascimento (Pelé)
Birth date	October 21, 1940
Place of birth	Tres Coracoes (Three Hearts), Brazil
Position	Center forward
Height	5'8"
Weight	145–165 pounds
Professional debut	1956
Retirement	1977

Appendix 2.   Professional History

World Cup Participation Brazil	1958, 1962, 1966, 1970
World Cup Champion	1958, 1962, 1970
Brazilian Team: Santos	1956–1974
U.S. Team: New York Cosmos	1975–1977

Appendix 3.   Notable Goals

Goal Number	Date	Game
1	September 7, 1956	Santos vs. Corinthians Santo Andre
100	July 27, 1958	Santos vs. Botafogo
500	September 5, 1962	Santos vs. Botafogo
1,000	November 12, 1969	Santos vs. Santa Cruze Recife
1,219	October 2, 1974	Santos vs. Ponte Preta (Pelé's final goal for Santos)
1,220	June 15, 1975	New York Cosmos vs. Dallas Tornados (Pelé's first North American Soccer League goal)
1,283	October 1, 1977	New York Cosmos vs. Santos (Pelé's final goal of his career)

Appendix 4.   Individual Worldwide Honors

Year	Honor
1970	BBC Sports Personality of the Year Overseas Personality
1981	Athlete of the 20th Century, poll by French daily newspaper, *L'Equipe*
1993	Inducted into American National Soccer Hall of Fame
1997	Awarded Knight Commander of the Order of the British Empire
1999	Athlete of the 20th Century, Reuters New Agency
1999	Athlete of the 20th Century, International Olympic Committee
1999	UNICEF Soccer Player of the 20th Century
1999	*Time* Magazine, One of the 100 Most Important People of the 20th Century
1999	International Federation of Football History and Statistics Soccer Player of the 20th Century
1999	Soccer Player of the 20th Century, selected by France Football's Golden Ball Winners
1999	International Federation of Football History and Statistics, South American Soccer Player of the 20th Century

(*Continued*)

Appendix 4. (*Continued*)

Year	Honor
1999	Soccer Player of the 20th Century, selected by France Football's Golden Ball Winners
1999	International Federation of Football History and Statistics, South American Soccer Player of the 20th Century
2000	Fédération Internationale de Football Association (FIFA) Player of the 20th Century
2000	Lareus World Sports Awards Lifetime Achievement Award from South African president Nelson Mandela
2005	BBC Sports Personality of the Year Lifetime Achievement Award
2012	Greatest Soccer Player in History, Golden Foot

BIBLIOGRAPHY

BOOKS

Gutman, Bill. *Pelé*. New York: Grosset & Dunlap, 1976.

Harris, Harry. *Pelé: His Life and Times*. New York: Welcome Rain Publishers, 2001.

Kowet, Don. *Pelé*. New York: Atheneum, 1976.

Marcus, Joe. *The World of Pelé*. New York: Mason/Charter, 1976.

(No name). *Pelé*. West Haven, CT: Academic Industries, Inc., 1984.

Pelé. *10: What Makes a Great Player from the Master*. Newbury Park, CA: Haynes Publishing, 2010.

Pelé. *My Life in Pictures*. New York: Simon & Schuster, 2008.

Pelé and Fish, Robert L. *My Life and the Beautiful Game*. New York: Doubleday & Company, 1977.

Thebaud, François. *Pelé*. New York: Harper & Row Publishers, 1976.

MAGAZINES

Axthelm, Pete. "The Most Famous Athlete in the World." *Sports Illustrated*, October 24, 1966.

Terrell, Roy. "Viva Vava and Garrincha!" *Sports Illustrated*, June 25, 1962.

NEWSPAPERS

Eskenazi, Gerald. "Prospects for Cosmos Take a Bullish Turn." *The New York Times*, June 5, 1975.

Howe, Marvine, "Pelé Out to Sway U.S. Fans." *The New York Times*, June 5, 1975.

Montgomery, Paul. "Pelé Signs with Cosmos: 'Soccer Has Arrived' Here." *The New York Times*, June 12, 1975.

"Soccer's Superlative: Edson Arantes do Nascimento." *The New York Times*, June 4, 1975.

Winter, Henry. "Pelé in Britain to Help Brazil's Push for Elusive Gold against Mexico at Wembley." *London Telegraph*, August 9, 2012.

Yannis, Alex. "Pelé: A Slim Figure of Athletic Perfection." *The New York Times*, June 10, 1975.

Yannis, Alex. "21,278 See Pelé Score and Cosmos Tie." *The New York Times*, June 16, 1975.

Yannis, Alex. "Cosmos Demand More Security for Pelé." *The New York Times*, June 22, 1975.

Yannis, Alex. "Cosmos: Experiment that Failed." *The New York Times*, August 5, 1975.

WEBSITES ABOUT PELÉ

http://www.pele-sports.com
https://twitter.com/Pele
www.facebook.com/Pele
www.latinosportslegends.com/Pele_bio.htm

INDEX

About the Author

Lew Freedman is the author of more than 60 books, mostly about sports and Alaska. A veteran newspaperman for such publications as the *Anchorage Daily News*, the *Philadelphia Inquirer*, and the *Chicago Tribune*, Freedman is the winner of more than 250 journalism awards. He and his wife Debra live in Indiana.